M

MW00893480

Cookbooks

~ The Basics ~

An Introduction To Cooking

by

Geoff & Vicky Wells

Published by Geezer Guides

Copyright© 2012 Geoff & Vicky Wells

~~~

CONTENTS

WELCOME TO YOUR FIRST COOKBOOK

Cooking is basically easy. All you do is mix some stuff together and heat it up. The items you mix together are called ingredients. A recipe tells you how to mix the ingredients and how long to heat them.

There are thousands and thousands of recipes that tell you the ingredients and the method to make every delicious food you can think of.

There is a kind of secret language that is used in most recipes that you will need to learn. It's not scary and the words are mostly all in English, but each of these special words means you have to do things in a particular way. We have included a glossary that explains all these cooking terms, at least all we could think of.

Out of the thousands of recipes there are, we have chosen the ones in this book because they are fun, delicious and a great introduction to cooking. We have tried to select recipes where you will use a variety of skills that will be useful to you for the rest of your life.

You don't have to make these recipes in any particular order - just choose any one you like and get started. However, we do suggest you read through the entire book at least once because we have included many tips you might otherwise miss.

IS THIS A REAL COOKBOOK?

Absolutely, these are real recipes just like you find in any other cookbook. The difference is that we go into much more detail explaining how to make each dish. We have also specially selected each recipe to demonstrate some particular technique.

INGREDIENTS

We don't use abbreviations in any of our cookbooks but many authors will specify tsp instead of teaspoon or tbs instead of tablespoon, so be careful when reading the measurements in other recipes. Also it is a convention of cookbooks that ingredients are listed in the order you use them. This is not always the case with recipes you find online.

This book is written using North American measurements but to make it useful for metric users we have included an appendix of conversions for quantities and temperatures.

KITCHEN SAFETY

Accidents happen and around the home and the kitchen is frequently where they happen the most. It's important that you learn to recognise the dangers and do what you can to minimise the risks. Each recipe in this book will include a section on any possible danger. We are certainly not trying to scare you, we just want to point out the dangers that you might not have thought about without previous experience.

DON'T BURN YOURSELF

When you cook, things get hot, so you must be careful not to burn yourself. You should always have an adult in the kitchen with you when you are cutting or heating anything.

Make sure you have properly fitting oven mitts before you try to take anything out of the oven or lift a saucepan lid. If your hands are still small, don't try to use oven mitts made for an adult because they won't give you the control you need.

ABOUT KNIVES

You might think this is odd but the safest knife is the sharpest one. If a knife is dull you have to push hard to make it cut. When you push hard that is when you lose control and you cut fingers instead of vegetables.

Get into the habit of sharpening your knives before you start to cook anything. You can get stand alone electric knife sharpeners and sometimes they are built in to the back of your can opener. Personally, we prefer the hand units that have two sets of wheels and you draw the blade between them. If you draw the blade across the wheels a couple of times every day you will keep a nice sharp edge on your knife.

There are many shapes and different types of specialty knives but two or three is all you need to get started.

CHEF'S KNIFE

Number one on your list should be what's called a chef's knife. This is an all purpose knife that comes in different sizes between 6 and 12 inches long.

The important design factor is the wide curved blade that allows you to rock it on the cutting board.

Paring Knife

The second most important knife is the paring knife. This is a small (between 3 and 6 inches) used for peeling, fine trimming and other intricate work.

Cleaver

Although not essential, a cleaver is one of those tools that if you need it, you really need it. It is used in a chopping motion and should only be used when your other hand is well out of the way. It will easily cut through meat bones and finger bones so use with great care.

Wikipedia

If you are interested in finding out more about the different types of knives and how to care for them search Wikipedia for "Kitchen Knife".

BREAKFAST

There are lots of really great things you can eat for breakfast but the sad truth is most people today don't have time to make them. They get up late and have to scramble around to get ready for work or school. Often a piece of toast or a bowl of sugary cereal is all they get.

It doesn't need to be that way of course. Just get up 15-20 minutes earlier and you can enjoy any of these healthy, tasty breakfast alternatives.

If you really can't find the time on a school day at least try to have something different on the weekends.

OATMEAL

You can get flavoured oatmeal in a one serving package that only needs you to pour on some boiling water but that is almost as bad as the sugary cereal.

Oatmeal is one of the best thing you can have for breakfast but to really get the benefit from it you need to start with the original variety. Oatmeal is sold in various versions based on the amount of time it takes to cook. If it is rolled thinner or chopped smaller it cooks faster.

SAFETY

You will be stirring a saucepan of boiling liquid. Make sure your saucepan has a handle that does not get hot because you will be holding the handle as you stir.

Depending on the type of stove you have you might be reaching to the back of the stove to adjust the heat of your burner. As you reach don't allow your arm to get near the steam from the oatmeal as steam can be very hot and could give you a nasty burn.

EQUIPMENT YOU NEED

Small saucepan
Measuring cup or measuring spoons
Wooden or plastic stirring spoon

SERVINGS

Single serving

SKILL

Measuring

INGREDIENTS

1 cup cold water
½ cup oatmeal
dash salt - optional
sugar - optional
milk or cream

Method

OK this is pretty basic but you have to start somewhere. One of the first cooking skills you need to learn is how to measure ingredients. For most recipes the quantities are fairly flexible but baking is an exception. For oatmeal you don't have to be precise, but you do have to be pretty close. The more oatmeal you have to water and the longer you cook it, the thicker the porridge will be.

Start by using a ratio of one part oatmeal to two parts water. If it's not the way you like it use more water or more oatmeal tomorrow.

If you put the oats and salt in the saucepan with cold water and bring it to a boil you will make creamier porridge. If you boil the water and salt first and then add the oats you will get chewier porridge. It depends on how you like it.

If you are using the "Old Fashioned" oats you cook them for about five minutes, if you use the "Quick Oats" you need only cook them for one minute.

Options

Vary the taste by adding different ingredients. Learn to experiment and see which foods go together and which ones don't. You are not likely to enjoy spinach with your oatmeal but raisins go nicely. You can also try combinations of apple, peach, cherry, cinnamon, almond, brown sugar or maple syrup.

MICROWAVE SCRAMBLED EGGS

Microwave ovens are very quick and they have lots of uses but they will never be our favorite choice for cooking anything - except for scrambled eggs. Turns out a microwave oven on low power is absolutely the best way to cook scrambled eggs.

SAFETY

In most cases with microwave cooking the food will cook but the non metallic dish you cook in does not get hot. This is not always the case so be careful particularly when long cooking times are involved.

Toast coming out of a toaster can be hot enough to burn. If the piece of toast is not big enough to stick up above the top of the toaster so you can grab it, don't try to stick a knife into the toaster to pry it out. There are wooden and silicon tongs available that are made specifically for removing toast from a toaster.

EQUIPMENT YOU NEED

4 cup oven safe measuring cup
Fork or whisk
Toaster

SERVINGS

2 servings

SKILL

Precise microwave timing and meal completion timing.

INGREDIENTS

4 eggs
pepper & salt to taste
4 slices whole wheat bread
4 pats butter

METHOD

Crack the eggs one by one on the side of the measuring cup and drop the white and yolk of the eggs into the measuring cup. Use a fork to whip the eggs together until they are covered in a light froth.

Put the measuring cup in the microwave and cook on low power for about eight minutes. Microwave ovens vary quite a bit in their power so we can't give you any exact cooking times. If you see any microwave recipe that gives you exact times watch what you are cooking very carefully the first time.

Microwave ovens have settings to adjust their power so that you can slow down the cooking process. To cook scrambled eggs you must use a low power setting or you will end up with a yellow rubber ball. Start by using ½ power or lower.

In our experience, the cooking time for four eggs is usually about eight minutes but the last minute is critical. Open the oven door every couple of minutes and stir the mixture with your fork. Your eggs are done when there is just a tiny bit of egg mixture left that appears uncooked. Take the measuring cup out of the microwave and whip the eggs again with your fork.

How long does your toaster take to make a slice of toast, about two minutes? Do you have a two slice or a four slice toaster? Use this information to figure out when you need to start cooking the toast so that everything is ready to eat at the same time.

EGG MCBREAKFAST

This fast food favorite is easy to make at home.

SAFETY

Due to the size of an English muffin they won't stick out above a regular toaster so you need to use a toaster oven where you can lay them down on the rack or a bagel toaster that lifts the muffin or bagel above the level of the slots.

Egg rings have an attached handle so you don't burn yourself when you remove them but with the home made kind you have to be more careful.

EQUIPMENT YOU NEED

Non-stick frying pan
Spatula - (egg flipper)
2 egg rings - you can buy an egg ring at any kitchen specialty store or you can make one by cutting the top and bottom off a tuna can. Just watch out for sharp edges on the can.
Bagel toaster or toaster oven

SERVINGS

2 servings

SKILL

Egg frying

INGREDIENTS

2 English muffins
2 teaspoons coconut or olive oil
2 medium or large eggs
2 slices ham cut to fit muffins
2 slices cheddar cheese

METHOD

If you don't cook an egg properly they can turn rubbery. The secret is to get the temperature of the frying pan just right which is between 325°F and

350°F. The egg should begin cooking as soon as it hits the pan but the pan shouldn't be so hot that the edge of the egg gets crispy.

If you have an egg ring, place it in the frying pan and let it warm up with the pan. It's not essential, all it does is keep the egg white in a circle so it fits properly on the muffin.

Experience is the best way to know when your frying pan is at the right temperature. Start by setting your burner to medium and giving your pan a minute or two to warm up.

Pour a ½ teaspoon of oil into the egg ring. If the oil just spreads slowly to the edges your pan is not hot enough. If the oil crackles, splashes and smokes it is too hot. When the temperature is right crack your egg and let the contents fall gently into the ring. It should start cooking right away. Once the white is set you can remove the ring. Some people like their eggs runny and some like them solid. There is no correct way but you don't want to overcook them.

It will probably take longer to toast your English muffin than to fry your eggs so you should get them in the toaster just before you start your eggs.

Put the two pieces of ham in the frying pan beside the eggs so they get warm and flip them over when you remove the egg rings.

Cheese slices are the easiest to use but for a better taste cut a few thin pieces from a block of real cheese.

There's no need to butter the muffin just layer the ham, cheese and egg.

PRESENTATION

Presentation means what you can do to make your food look as good as possible. Chef's will put almost as much effort into their presentation as they do to cooking. Try putting a couple of halves of a cherry tomato and a sprig of parsley on the plate beside the muffin. The red and green makes the muffin look more attractive.

WESTERN OMELET

SAFETY

You are going to be chopping ham and onions using a big knife so obviously you need to keep your fingers out of the way. If your hands are still small you should have an adult get things started because you just don't have enough grip strength to control the knife yet.

The most dangerous part is cutting the onion in half. You have to control the onion with one hand and the knife with the other. If the onion rolls while you are cutting you may find yourself cutting finger instead of onion.

Once the ham and onion are in large chunks you can take over to do the fine chopping.

Arrange the ham or onion chunks in the center of your chopping board. If you are right-handed touch the point of the knife on the left-hand side of the pile. Put the palm of you left hand on the back of the knife just up from the point. Now rock the knife down to the cutting board, cutting through whatever is below.

Keep doing this action over and over until everything is finely chopped. This means the food should be in little pieces no more than about ¼" on any side.

EQUIPMENT YOU NEED

> 9" Cast iron omelet pan
> Small bowl or measuring cup
> Fork or whisk
> Spatula (egg flipper)
> Toaster
> Chef's knife
> Chopping board

SERVINGS

> Serves 1

11

SKILL

Chopping

INGREDIENTS

½ medium onion
¼ cup chopped ham
2 teaspoons coconut or olive oil
2 eggs
2 slices toast

METHOD

Start by breaking the eggs into your measuring cup and whipping them with the fork or whisk. It's also a good idea to warm your serving plates so the food doesn't get cold. You can use hot water or put them in a very low oven - no more than 200°F.

Put your omelet pan on medium heat and give it a couple of minutes to warm up. A cast iron pan will take longer to heat than the thin aluminum kind. You can use any frying pan of course but an omelet pan just makes it easier because it is the right size.

Pour the oil into the pan and cook the onion until it turns clear. Set aside. (This just means remove the onion from the pan and put it in a dish for later.)

Pour the egg mixture into the pan and make sure it is evenly distributed in the pan. Cast iron pans are made in one piece so the handles can get pretty hot. You may need an oven mitt to hold it.

Quickly stir the mixture to make sure it all gets cooked. You only do this lightly because you're making an omelet not scrambled eggs. Spread the ham and onion evenly over the surface of the omelet.

Now would be a good time to get the toast started so that it will be ready when the omelet has finished cooking.

Use your spatula to scrape around the edges of the pan and check to see if it is done. The bottom should be a very light brown and it should release from the pan. Flip one half of the omelet over the other to make a "D" shape then slide it out onto the warm serving plate.

Alternatively you can gently slide half the omelet onto the plate then use the edge of the frying pan to fold the other half of the omelet to make the "D".

PRESENTATION

You can decorate the plate with orange and tomato slices to add some color but the real trick is getting the omelet fluffy and into the perfect "D" shape. It just takes practice.

MOSQUITO TOAST

Don't worry, there aren't any mosquitoes in the ingredients. This is just a version of French Toast that is eaten along the Mosquito Coast in Belize. Belize used to be called British Honduras and is just south of Cancun on the East coast of Mexico.

This recipe uses either mascarpone or ricotta cheese. They are both very light Italian cheeses somewhat like American cream cheese. You can substitute cream cheese if you want but it's more fun to explore all the different tastes from other cultures.

SAFETY

Other than the hot frying pan you don't really have anything to be concerned about with this recipe.

EQUIPMENT YOU NEED

Large heavy bottom frying pan.
Small dish or dessert plate
Measuring cup or bowl
Fork or whisk

SERVINGS

Serves 4

SKILL

Using spices and evenly coating bread with an egg mixture.

INGREDIENTS

8 slices raisin bread
½ cup mascarpone or ricotta cheese
1 teaspoon ground cinnamon, divided*
3 large eggs, beaten
½ cup heavy cream
1 teaspoon nutmeg, freshly grated
1 teaspoon vanilla extract (real vanilla, not artificial)

Butter for frying

*Divided in a recipe means that the quantity shown will be used in more than one place in the recipe. In this recipe the ingredient list calls for 1 teaspoon of cinnamon - ½ teaspoon is mixed with the cheese and the other ½ teaspoon is mixed with the egg and cream.

METHOD

Start by combining ½ teaspoon of ground cinnamon with the mascarpone or ricotta cheese. Combine is just another way of saying mix.

Now spread 4 slices of raisin bread with the cheese mixture and add the other 4 slices to make 4 cheese sandwiches.

In your measuring cup, combine the beaten eggs, heavy cream, remaining cinnamon, nutmeg and vanilla and mix well. The quantities of most ingredients in a recipe are fairly flexible but spices need to be measured more exactly. You may not necessarily agree with the amount of spice suggested and will adjust what the recipe calls for based on your own experience. However, the first time you cook a recipe it's a good idea to stick with the recipe.

Pour the mixture into a shallow dish like a dessert bowl then carefully lower each "sandwich" into the egg mixture allowing enough time for the bread to absorb some of the egg mixture. Turn each one over to make sure both sides are well coated.

On medium-high heat melt the butter in a large frying pan. Once the pan is hot and the butter is bubbling, place one (or two if the pan is large enough) of the "sandwiches" in the pan. Make sure each piece is in the butter because that is what will help brown the bread.

Be sure to cook each side long enough so that it is well done and completely heated through. You need to keep a close eye on the heat so that it doesn't burn before it is heated in the middle. If you think one side is burning flip it over and heat the other side.

Cut each "sandwich" into four triangles and arrange on a warm plate.

PRESENTATION

You can dress up this Mosquito Toast however you like. Here are just a few suggestions:

Tate & Lyle's Golden Syrup (a favorite in England)
Maple Syrup
Powdered Sugar
Whipped Cream
Fresh Berries (strawberries, raspberries, blueberries, etc)
Fresh Pineapple

Scratch Pancakes Or Waffles

We have never understood why anybody buys pancake mix. All it is is a mixture of flour, baking powder and powdered milk. It's really no easier or quicker than just making your own from scratch.

Safety

You're working with hot frying pans, waffle makers and oven so all the usual precautions apply. Use oven mitts sized to fit small hands to make sure you can get a proper grip.

Equipment You Need

Large bowl, or 4 cup measuring cup
Fork or whisk
Frying pan, griddle or waffle maker
Spatula (egg flipper)

Servings

Serves 4

Skill

Measuring

There is a lot of chemistry going on in the kitchen, which is most apparent when you do any kind of baking. You need to be very careful with quantities otherwise the recipes just won't work. Ingredients like sugar, salt, baking powder, eggs and milk all have a specific job to do. When you understand the chemistry of food you can substitute different ingredients that do the same job but until then stick with the recipe.

Ingredients

2 cups all purpose flour
2½ teaspoons baking powder
3 tablespoons sugar
½ teaspoon salt
2 large eggs

1½ cups milk

Olive oil
2 tablespoons olive oil for pancakes
½ cup olive oil for waffles

METHOD

In a large bowl, or 4 cup measuring cup, combine the flour, baking powder, sugar and salt. Mix well.

In a separate bowl, or 4 cup measuring cup, beat the eggs and add the milk and olive oil (2 tablespoons if you're making pancakes or ½ cup if you're making waffles). Mix well.

The pancake and waffle mixtures are the same except the waffle mixture contains a lot more oil so that it will release from the machine.

Note: if you want thinner pancakes, add a little more milk.

Pour the liquid ingredients into the flour mixture and stir only until well mixed. Do not over mix.

Pancakes

Heat a large skillet or griddle, greased with some olive oil (or other vegetable oil), over a medium-high heat. Once it's hot, reduce the heat to medium.

Pour about ¼ cup of batter for each pancake onto the hot skillet or griddle.

Wait for a lot of bubbles to form on the top of each pancake before you turn them over. Turn the pancakes over only once. Use your spatula to lift the edge to check when they are done. They cook quickly so don't let them burn.

Keep the completed pancakes warm in a 190°F - 200°F oven on a pre-warmed plate until you have cooked them all.

Waffles

Waffle makers vary so follow the manufacturer's instructions. Just be careful not to use so much batter that it pours over the sides of the machine.

PRESENTATION

Serve with butter and your favorite syrup. Or you can get more creative and add fresh fruit like strawberries or blueberries. Ice cream or whipped cream or both also make great additions to pancakes or waffles.

LUNCH

Other than weekends most of your lunchtime will, most likely, be spent at work or school. So with that in mind we'll start with a couple of hot lunches you can make on the weekend then go on to things you can pack in your lunch box.

Easy Sloppy Joes

Safety

Kitchen safety isn't just about getting cut or burned, it's also about hygiene. You will use your hands a lot so make it a practice to wash your hands before starting to prepare any food. You've probably seen pictures of what surgeons go through before an operation and we are not suggesting you need to be that thorough but be sure to include the back of your hands and your wrists.

Equipment You Need

Large frying pan or skillet
Sieve or colander

Servings

Serves 4

Skill

Removing and handling unwanted fat

Ingredients

1 pound ground beef, lean
½ cup chopped onion
¼ cup green bell pepper, chopped
¼ cup celery, chopped
¼ cup mushrooms, sliced
1 tablespoon vinegar
1½ teaspoons Worcestershire sauce
¼ cup ketchup
1 can tomato soup
Salt & pepper, to taste
4 hamburger buns

Method

In a large skillet over medium heat, brown the hamburger. Drain the meat in a colander lined with paper towel. Never pour grease or fat down the drain as it will cool and solidify almost immediately and clog your drain. This recipe uses a can of tomato soup so you can pour the extra grease into the empty can and put it into the garbage after it sets.

While the meat is draining, add the onions to the small amount of grease left in the skillet and cook until translucent.

Return the hamburger to the skillet with the onions and add the rest of the ingredients, (except for the hamburger buns). Continue to cook over medium heat until the celery is tender - about 5 minutes.

Note: If you prefer, you can substitute 1½ cups of barbecue sauce for the ketchup and tomato soup.

Divide the mixture into 4 portions and spread on the hamburger bun bottoms.

Note: If you like, you can top each Sloppy Joe with a little shredded cheese before you add the bun tops.

PRESENTATION

French fries or home fries may be more than you want to eat for lunch but a few potato chips, lettuce leaves and a slice or two of tomato will help to dress up the plate.

MEXICAN STYLE SLOW COOKER BAKED BEANS

SAFETY

If you are strong enough you can hold the saucepan in one hand and the lid in the other as you drain the beans by holding the lid so that only the water can pour from the saucepan.

The safer way is to use a colander to drain the beans.

EQUIPMENT YOU NEED

Measuring cup
4 quart saucepan

SERVINGS

Serves 16

SKILL

Safely draining liquid from hot foods.

INGREDIENTS

16 ounces dried navy beans
10 cups water
1 can diced tomatoes, 28 ounces
1 can black beans, 15 ounces
1 can Mexican-style whole kernel corn, 10 ounces
2 tablespoons taco seasoning mix
½ cup onion, chopped
1 teaspoon chili powder

METHOD

In a 4 quart saucepan, combine the water and the 16 ounces of dried navy beans. Heat to boiling. Reduce heat to low and simmer, covered, for one hour, then drain.

Drain the canned black beans and the canned Mexican-style corn.

22

Combine all the ingredients in a slow cooker and mix well.

Set the slow cooker to low and cook for 6 to 7 hours.

Stir well and serve.

PRESENTATION

Put a single serving in a small bowl and top with shredded cheddar cheese, salsa and sour cream.

No-Fuss Baked Mac & Cheese

Safety

Be sure you are wearing well fitting oven mitts and know where you are going to put the hot dish before you remove it from the oven.

Equipment You Need

Measuring cup
2 quart oven-proof casserole dish

Servings

Serves 6

Skill

Melting butter in the oven and shredding cheese.

Ingredients

3 tablespoons butter
2½ cups uncooked macaroni
1 teaspoon sea salt
½ teaspoon black pepper, freshly ground
8 ounces cheddar cheese, shredded
4 cups milk

Method

Pre-heat the oven to 350°F.

Place the butter in a 2 quart, oven-proof casserole dish. Place the dish in the oven until the butter melts.

Carefully remove the casserole from the oven and stir in the uncooked macaroni. Toss to coat the macaroni with the melted butter.

Sprinkle with salt, pepper and the shredded cheese. Toss to mix the cheese in.

Carefully pour the milk over everything in the casserole dish but DON'T stir it.

Return to the oven and bake, uncovered, at 350°F for 1 hour.

Remove from the oven and allow to cool slightly on a wire rack before serving.

PRESENTATION

Serve as a complete lunch or with meat and a vegetable as a side dish.

PIGGIES IN A BLANKET

We've seen many recipes that call themselves "Piggies in a Blanket" but none that are right, as far as we are concerned. We have always believed that this recipe must have pork breakfast sausages and real pastry.

SAFETY

Don't forget that on most ovens you fold the oven door down to open it. When you reach for the food you are reaching over the very hot oven door. If you are small the distance you have to reach and the weight of the food could easily overbalance you. Be very careful.

EQUIPMENT YOU NEED

Frying pan or skillet
Large baking sheet

SERVINGS

Serves 24

SKILL

Rolling and cutting pastry.

INGREDIENTS

8 ounces pork breakfast sausage, cooked
pastry dough, enough for a 1 crust pie

METHOD

Remove the pork breakfast sausages from their package and cook them in the skillet over a medium heat until they are lightly browned.

Remove the sausages to a plate lined with paper towel to absorb any excess fat and allow the cooked sausages to cool to room temperature. Cut each sausage in half so that it is 1½ to 2 inches long.

Pre-heat the oven to 400°F.

Chill the pastry dough and then roll it out on a lightly floured surface using a chilled rolling pin. Roll the dough to about ⅛ inch thick. Then cut the dough with either a knife or a pizza cutter. Cut it into strips just slightly narrower than the length of the sausages (you want a bit of sausage to peak out at each end), and just long enough to wrap around the sausage with a bit of an overlap.

Wrap the pastry around each sausage half and place them, seam side down, on a slightly greased baking sheet.

Bake at 400°F. for approximately 10-15 minutes or until the pastry is nicely browned.

Remove from the oven and cool on a wire rack.

PRESENTATION

Arrange on a serving plate with tomato wedges and sweet pickles.

HAM AND CHEESE WRAPS

SAFETY

Most people seem to think that mayonnaise will go bad very quickly but, in fact, this is not true. Home made mayonnaise should be consumed within a day or two and should be refrigerated but the commercial stuff does not need to be refrigerated at all.

EQUIPMENT YOU NEED

Butter knife
Plastic wrap

SERVINGS

Serves 2

SKILL

Learning how to fold and roll sandwich wraps.

INGREDIENTS

2 large whole wheat tortillas, about 8"
1 tablespoon mayonnaise, optional
1 tablespoon mustard, optional
2 lettuce leaves
2 slices cooked ham
2 slices swiss cheese

METHOD

Place the whole wheat, soft tortillas on a flat surface. If you are using the mayonnaise and/or mustard, spread ½ tablespoon on each tortilla.

Place a lettuce leaf, a slice of swiss cheese and a slice of ham on each tortilla.

Fold up about one quarter of the the tortilla. Then, from one side, roll the tortilla. This way you get a closed bottom and an open top.

Wrap each completed tortilla sandwich tightly in plastic wrap so it stays fresh until lunch time.

PRESENTATION

You may want to include some tomato wedges in a separate baggie. It's best not to put tomato on any kind of sandwich that is not eaten right away as it will make the bread soggy.

Chicken in a Pocket

Safety

Using a sharp knife to cut up evenly sized pieces of food is not like chopping because your fingers are much closer to the blade. Keep control of your knife at all times.

Equipment You Need

Servings

Serves 2

Skill

Gently opening a pita to create a pocket.

Ingredients

1 whole wheat pita, about 6"
1 cup cooked chicken, cubed
2 tablespoons mayonnaise
1 stalk celery, chopped
½ cup seedless grapes, cut in half, optional
4 lettuce leaves
4 tomato slices

Method

Cut the pita bread in half and, gently open the pita with a dull knife, making two pockets.

Combine the chicken, mayonnaise, celery and grapes (if using) in a medium bowl and toss well.

Place two lettuce leaves (you can use Romaine, iceberg or any type of leaf lettuce) in each pita half, lining the pocket.

Place two tomato slices in each pita half. Try to get them against the lettuce. Cut tomato in a sandwich can make bread soggy if the sandwich is not eaten right away. Pita is not as likely to be affected, particularly if the lettuce leaf is shielding it from the tomato juice.

Place half of the chicken mixture in each pita pocket.

Wrap tightly with plastic wrap so it will stay fresh until lunch time.

PRESENTATION

If you wrap the pita in a paper towel before the plastic wrap you will have a way of catching any possible drips while you are eating it.

APPETIZERS

Appetizers are also called hors d'oeuvres, tapas or starters. They can be served as the first course in a meal to stimulate the appetite or a variety of them are served at a cocktail party as the only food.

You may not be giving cocktail parties for a few more years but it is still nice to have some snacks prepared for when friends come over.

CELERY PLUS

Simple, yet versatile, there's nothing like the crunch of fresh celery. It lends itself to all kinds of fillings, making it a great but very simple appetizer. Here are just a few suggestions for this popular veggie.

SAFETY

The only thing you have to be careful about is chopping the celery and not your fingers

EQUIPMENT YOU NEED

Chef's knife
Chopping board
Serving platter

SKILL

How to keep celery fresh (see the tip below).

INGREDIENTS

1 bunch celery
cream cheese
liverwurst
peanut butter
paté, any kind
salsa, medium or hot, drained
garlic, finely minced
fresh parsley, finely minced
mascarpone cheese
sharp, cold-pack cheese
egg salad
salmon salad
tuna salad
chicken salad

METHOD

Preparing the Celery

Choose a fresh, crispy bunch of celery.

Break each stalk off of the bunch and wash thoroughly.

Cut into 2-3 pieces. Or fill the celery cavity first and then cut it.

Retain the pieces with the leaves to use as garnish on this, or other dishes.

Tip

As soon as you get celery home from the store break it apart and stand it in water. A plastic juice jug works well for this purpose. If you keep the jug and the celery in the fridge it will stay fresh and crisp for a long time. If you don't keep it in water it will quickly go limp and will only be good for cooking.

Stuffing the Celery

As we mentioned above, there are all kinds of tasty items that you can use to fill celery.

The items in the ingredients list are some of our favorites and some of them can be combined as well.

For example, you can mix salsa (well drained) or freshly minced garlic with the cream cheese, the liverwurst or the mascarpone (a very smooth textured cheese).

Pre-made egg, salmon, tuna or chicken salad make a great stuffing.

I'm sure you can come up with many other ideas as well.

PRESENTATION

You can prepare a serving platter with a selection of fillings or you can use the celery pieces as garnish between other appetizers.

CHEESE AND JALAPENO BREAD STICKS

This is the most complicated recipe in the book, but the results are worth the effort. To make things easier, you can prepare the bread dough in a bread machine, just follow the instructions on your bread maker for the order of the ingredients. You could put the cheese and Jalapeno in at the add-ins beep, but we suggest you knead them in later, after the dough is done so they don't get too chopped up by the bread machine.

SAFETY

As always when working with a hot oven be sure to wear well fitting oven mitts and be careful when reaching over the oven door.

EQUIPMENT YOU NEED

Large mixing bowl
Clean smooth surface - preferably marble or granite
Kitchen scale
Baking sheet
Large baking dish
Small dish or measuring cup
Pastry brush

SERVINGS

Serves 36

SKILL

How to proof yeast when making bread from scratch.

INGREDIENTS

2 cups warm water
2 tablespoons sugar
2 tablespoons active dry yeast
2 cups rye flour
1 tablespoon sea salt
2 tablespoons olive oil
2 cups unbleached white flour

2 cups cheddar cheese, grated (about 4 ounces) divided
¼ cup jalapeno peppers, chopped
1 egg

METHOD

In a large bowl, mix together the warm water and sugar, then sprinkle on the active dry yeast. Set the bowl aside for 5-10 minutes to proof. (See glossary under "proof")

After this amount of time there should be a somewhat foamy top on the water (that's the yeast). If this is not the case then your water was either too cold or too hot, or the yeast is no longer good. If that is the case you need to throw this out and start again.

Add the olive oil, salt and the 2 cups of rye flour. Beat with an electric mixer on medium-low speed for 3 minutes.

If your electric mixer has dough hooks, switch to those and gradually beat in 1½ cups of the unbleached flour. Mix until you have a sticky dough.

Turn out onto a floured surface and knead in the remaining ½ cup of unbleached flour. Be careful not to add too much, you don't want the dough to be dry.

Gradually knead in about 1¼ cups of the shredded cheese and the chopped jalapeno peppers. Add just a little at a time and knead until incorporated, then add more until all the cheese and jalapenos are incorporated. It is likely that you will need to add a bit more flour, just be sure not to add to much.

Continue to knead for another 5 minutes.

Transfer the dough to a warm, slightly-oiled bowl and turn the dough in the bowl to make sure the dough gets a light coating of oil.

Cover and allow to rise in a warm place for about 1 hour or until the dough has doubled in size.

Hint: an oven with just the oven light turned on is about the perfect temperature for dough to rise.

Once dough has doubled in size, punch it down (see glossary) and divide into 1½ ounces pieces. (If you don't have a kitchen scale, just try to divide the dough into 30-36 equal pieces.)

Roll each piece into a ball between the palms of your hands. Then roll each ball into a rope shape about 7 inches to 8 inches long. They will be pretty thin. Don't forget they're going to rise once more.

Transfer the "ropes" to a lightly greased baking sheet.

Cover and let rise in a warm place for about 45 minutes, or until they have doubled in size..

To help make the bread sticks crusty put a dish of water on the bottom rack of the oven and pre-heat the oven to 400°F. When you are finished baking leave the dish of water in the oven to cool before you remove it because the hot water could slosh around and spill onto your hands.

Once the bread sticks have doubled in size, in a small dish, beat the egg well and add about 1 tablespoon of water to make an egg wash.

With a pastry brush, brush the egg wash over the bread sticks.

Then sprinkle the remaining ¾ cup of grated cheese over the bread sticks

Bake at 400°F. for 8-12 minutes, or until the bread sticks are nicely browned and the cheese is melted and slightly browned.

Because they are so thin they are going to bake quickly. Ovens vary in temperature, so start watching them closely after about 5 minutes.

Remove from the oven and cool on a wire rack.

PRESENTATION

Place the bread sticks in three or four tumblers which you then put in several locations on your display table.

SALADS

Even a salad bar in a fast food restaurant can give you ideas for what you can do with fresh, raw vegetables. You can make salads to complement a meal or as a meal in itself.

Salads are great for anyone watching their weight because they are full of vitamins and nutrients plus within reason, you can eat as much as you like depending on the dressings.

Basic Chef Salad

Sometimes you may order a chef salad in a restaurant and get a bowl of lettuce and maybe a wedge of tomato. That really isn't very interesting so try to add more variety.

A chef salad is generally used as a complement to a main meal that may not include a green vegetable.

Safety

This is not a safety issue but there is a common myth that you shouldn't cut lettuce with a metal knife because it turns the lettuce brown. Regardless of whether you use a metal or plastic knife or just tear it with your hands the lettuce will start to turn brown after ten days or so. The simple solution is to not cut it until you are ready to eat it.

Equipment You Need

Salad spinner
4 salad bowls
Chef's knife
Cutting board

Servings

Serves 4

Skill

Peeling a hard boiled egg

Ingredients

1 head romaine lettuce
2 medium tomatoes, cut into wedges
2 hard-boiled eggs, cut into wedges
½ red or green bell pepper, diced
2 slices cooked bacon, crumbled
2 ounces shredded sharp cheddar or crumbled blue cheese
various salad dressings, to taste

METHOD

Wash the lettuce well and tear into bite-size pieces. Place the pieces in a salad spinner or pat them dry using paper towel

Distribute the lettuce evenly to the 4 salad bowls and top with equal amounts of the remaining ingredients.

Serve with salad dressings of your choice.

PRESENTATION

Although you can use an ordinary dessert bowl as a salad bowl, wooden salad bowls are inexpensive and make an attractive addition to your dinnerware.

HOW TO MAKE HARD BOILED EGGS

If you are lucky enough to have access to farm fresh eggs you will find they don't peel as easily as eggs that have been in the fridge for a week or so. You might want to use the oldest ones for hard boiling.

Put the number of eggs you want to cook in a saucepan and cover them with COLD water. The colder the better if you just took the eggs from the fridge. You really want the eggs and the water to be at the same temperature because you want the eggs and water to heat up at the same rate. This is to prevent the eggs from cracking. Put a teaspoon of salt in the water so that if the eggs should crack the salt will help to seal it.

Bring the water to a rolling boil then take the saucepan off the heat. Put a lid on the saucepan and let it sit for up to fifteen minutes. Less if you prefer a softer hard boiled egg.

When the time is up cool the eggs as quickly as possible by running them under cold water. You can even put some ice cubes in the water.

When the eggs are completely cooled you should be able to crack the shell and easily remove it. There is a very thin membrane between the egg and the shell which causes the problem when trying to cleanly peel the egg. It often helps to peel the egg under running water so the water gets under the membrane.

COBB SALAD WITH A TEX-MEX FLAIR

The original Cobb Salad was introduced by Robert Cobb at the Brown Derby restaurant in Los Angeles. There are many variations but basically you are combining chicken, cheese, bacon and eggs with lettuce, tomato and other usual salad ingredients. Some recipes also include ham.

It makes a very complete meal.

SAFETY

Just the usual cautions when working with sharp knives.

EQUIPMENT YOU NEED

Chef's knife
Chopping board
Salad spinner
Measuring cup
Small saucepan to hard boil the eggs. (See the Basic Chef Salad recipe)

SERVINGS

Serves 4

SKILL

Assembling and arranging a large salad.

INGREDIENTS

1 head Romaine lettuce, torn into bite-size pieces
1 head Boston lettuce, torn into bite-size pieces
4 hard boiled eggs, cut into wedges
2 cooked chicken breast, sliced
1 can black beans, (15 oz.) drained and rinsed
1 cup pepper jack cheese, shredded
12 slices bacon, cooked and crumbled
2 avocados, sliced and dipped in lemon juice
2 cups cherry tomatoes, cut in half

⅔ cup Ranch dressing
⅓ cup Salsa

METHOD

Wash the lettuce and spin or pat it dry. Arrange the torn lettuce leaves on the bottom of a large platter or 9" x 13" glass baking dish.

On top of the lettuce bed, arrange the chicken, eggs, black beans, cheese, bacon, avocados and cherry tomatoes in individual rows.

In a 2 cup measuring cup, combine the Ranch dressing and salsa. Mix well and pour evenly over the salad prior to serving.

PRESENTATION

Usually a Cobb salad is served tossed in a large bowl but the colors and variety of ingredients can be used to make very attractive geometric patterns on a plate.

Waldorf Salad

As you might guess from the name this salad was first served at the Waldorf Hotel in New York City. It has been around for over a hundred years and during that time there have been several variations. This version adds grapes to the traditional recipe but otherwise it is close to the original.

Safety

If you don't own an apple corer you will find it much easier to remove the core if you first cut the apple into four wedges and then use a paring knife to cut out the seeds.

Equipment You Need

Paring knife or apple corer
Chef's knife
Mixing bowl
Whisk

Servings

Serves 2

Skill

Coring fruit.

Ingredients

½ cup walnuts, chopped
½ cup celery, thinly sliced across the width of the stalk
½ cup red seedless grapes, cut in half
1 red apple, cored and chopped
3 tablespoons mayonnaise
1 tablespoon lemon juice, freshly squeezed
½ teaspoon sea salt
¼ teaspoon black pepper, freshly ground
6-8 lettuce leaves

METHOD

In a medium bowl, mix together, using a whisk, the mayonnaise and lemon juice.

Add the salt and pepper and mix.

Add the apple, celery, grapes and walnuts. Mix well.

PRESENTATION

Line two individual serving size salad bowls with lettuce leaves and place the apple mixture on top.

Easy, Tasty Taco Salad

Safety

Never pour hot grease into a plastic container because it will melt.

Equipment You Need

Frying pan or skillet
Spatula
Chef's knife
Chopping board
Slotted spoon
Measuring cup
4 dinner plates

Servings

Serves 4

Skill

Safely disposing of hot grease.

Keep an empty tin can that you can use to pour hot grease into. When it has cooled and solidified you can put it into the garbage.

Ingredients

1 pound lean ground beef
1 onion, chopped
Taco seasoning mix, approximately. 2 tablespoons
¼ cup water
8 cups romaine lettuce, torn
2 tomatoes, chopped
1 cup cheddar cheese, shredded
2 cups tortilla chips, coarsely crushed
½ cup sour cream
¼ cup jalapeno pepper, sliced (optional)

METHOD

In a large skillet on medium-high heat, brown the ground beef. Remove the beef from the pan with a slotted spoon and set aside.

Pour most of the fat into an old tin can and in the small amount of fat remaining in the skillet, fry the chopped onion until it is translucent.

Leaving the onion in the skillet, return the drained ground beef to the skillet, add the taco seasoning and the water and bring the mixture to a boil. Reduce the heat to medium-low and simmer for 3-4 minutes. The liquid in the pan will thicken.

Distribute the torn Romaine lettuce between four plates.

Top each plate of lettuce with ¼ of the meat mixture, chopped tomatoes, shredded cheese and crushed tortilla chips.

Place a dollop of sour cream on top of each salad and sprinkle with sliced jalapeno peppers, if desired.

PRESENTATION

Try to arrange the ingredients attractively on the plate. You might make a ring of lettuce around the outside of the plate then put the ground beef in the center. Add the tomato and sour cream to the center and sprinkle the tortilla and cheese on the lettuce.

Colorful Potato Salad

Safety

If you use homemade mayonnaise you need to keep the potato salad refrigerated and eat it within a couple of days. Commercial mayonnaise does not require refrigeration.

Equipment You Need

Large serving bowl
Mixing bowl or measuring cup

Servings

Serves 8

Skill

Quickly cooling food to stop the cooking process.

Ingredients

8 medium potatoes, with skins, cooked and diced
1½ cups mayonnaise
2 tablespoons apple cider vinegar
1 teaspoon sea salt
1 tablespoon dijon mustard
1 teaspoon fresh garlic, chopped
2 tablespoons green relish
½ teaspoon black pepper, freshly ground
2 celery stalks, sliced
1 cup red onion, chopped
5 hard-boiled eggs, chopped
Paprika

Method

Boil the potatoes in salted water until just fork-tender. Drain and cover with cold water to stop the cooking process. Drain again and allow to cool to room temperature.

Dice the potatoes into medium-size chunks and place in a large bowl.

In a separate bowl or measuring cup, mix together the mayonnaise, vinegar, mustard, salt, garlic, green relish and pepper.

Add the mayonnaise mixture to the potatoes and mix well.

Next, add the celery and onions to the potatoes and mix well.

Add the chopped eggs to the potato mixture and mix again.

Note: If you prefer, you can cut the eggs into wedges and arrange them on the top of the potato salad.

PRESENTATION

You may want to start by lining your serving bowl with a few lettuce leaves and then placing the completed potato salad on top. This would require an additional mixing bowl.

Finish the salad by sprinkling a little paprika on the top.

SOUPS

Homemade soups are easy to make, nutritious and mostly diet friendly. Commercially made soups are loaded with salt and other chemicals that make them a poor choice.

THICK VEGETABLE SOUP

This is a hearty soup you can eat for lunch or as a first course for supper. It's great for anyone on a diet as you can eat as much as you like without worrying too much about fat and calories. In fact if you eat a small bowl half an hour before supper you will be much less likely to overeat.

ABOUT BOUILLON

Years ago cooks would boil bones for hours to make stock. Stock is the starting point for soups, stews, gravies and sauces. Today we still boil ham bones and turkey carcasses but for most of our stock we turn to bouillon cubes, packages and tetra packs. Bouillon cubes are just concentrated stock.

Don't try to save money by buying dollar store bouillon cubes, they are loaded with salt. Stick with good brand names like OXO, Bovril, and Knorr.

SAFETY

This recipe contains rutabagas (also known as swede) which, in our opinion, is the most dangerous vegetable to prepare. That may sound silly, it's not like "Attack Of The Killer Rutabagas" but it is the fact that they are large and very hard to cut. The tendency is to put a lot of pressure on the knife just to cut them, then suddenly the vegetable splits and you lose control of the knife.

The safest way to cut them is to give them a good whack with a cleaver to cut them in half - keep your fingers well out of the way. Once they are in half you have a flat side you can lay them on and use the rocking chef's knife technique, we describe in the Toasted Western recipe, to cut them into cubes.

EQUIPMENT YOU NEED

Colander or sieve
Cleaver
Chef's knife
Cutting board
Plastic or wooden spoon

2 quart saucepan with lid
6 quart dutch oven or soup pot with lid

SERVINGS

10-12 large servings

SKILL

Making soup is a skill

INGREDIENTS

1 cup yellow split peas
¼ cup brown rice
1 cup carrots (2 large)
1 cup parsnips (2 large)
1 cup onion (1 large)
1 cup rutabagas (½ medium)
4 cups cabbage - coarsely chopped
4 cups cauliflower - coarsely chopped
4 cups broccoli - coarsely chopped
¼ cup red pepper - chopped
10 cups water - divided
4 tablespoonsful beef Bovril
1 package OXO beef bouillon
1 package OXO chicken bouillon

METHOD

You make this soup in two batches because the yellow split peas take so long to cook.

Start by rinsing 4 cups of yellow split peas in cold water. Drain into a colander or sieve then pour into a 2 quart saucepan with a good fitting lid. Add 4 cups of cold water and bring to a boil. Turn the heat to low and allow to simmer for about 2 hours.

You will need to watch carefully until you have your simmer temperature adjusted just right. Split peas can easily boil over and make a real mess on your stove.

You cook the peas until the mixture is smooth. They will have absorbed most of the water so you might have to stir for the last little while so they don't burn on the bottom of the saucepan. Choose a saucepan with a thick bottom so this is less likely to happen.

You can continue to make the soup or put the cooled peas in the fridge until the next day.

The second stage begins by cooking ¼ cup of brown rice in a cup of water for half an hour. Just bring the water to a boil and let it simmer.

Now you add the root vegetables because they take longer to cook than the greens. Carrots, parsnips, rutabagas and onions plus the remaining water (5 cups). Bring it to a simmer and cook for ten minutes. Add the cabbage, broccoli, cauliflower and red pepper and cook for another 10 minutes.

You now have a nourishing soup but it doesn't have very much flavour because we started with water instead of stock. Go ahead and taste it.

The next step is to add some flavour using bouillon cubes. We have specified Bovril and both beef and chicken OXO but the truth is it doesn't matter. Use what you have but add it slowly and each time be sure to taste it. You can always add more but once its added you can't take it back.

You still have the split pea mixture which will add lots of flavour and also thicken your soup. Add the bouillon sparingly until after you have added the split peas.

Soup often tastes better the second day after the flavours have had a chance to develop so you can either eat it now or put it in the fridge until tomorrow.

What Else Can You Do?

Don't get hung up trying to follow recipes exactly - use them as a suggestion. You will learn which ingredients are important and which ones you can substitute.

In this recipe the split peas are important because they provide basis for the stock. Carrots and onions are basic items for a vegetable soup but if you left out the red pepper it wouldn't really make much difference. Same goes for the other vegetables. Try adding turnips, asparagus, pea pods, bok choy, potatoes, yams the choices are endless.

Try putting a few servings in a blender and making a smooth soup. This could also become a sauce or gravy for a meal of sausages or hamburger patties for example. Just use your imagination.

Presentation

Serve a small portion as the first course to the evening meal to stimulate the appetite.

Chicken and Tortellini Soup

This a quick, tasty soup that's easy to make and a great alternative to the regular chicken noodle soup from a can.

Safety

As usual be careful when using sharp knives and boiling water.

Equipment You Need

Chef's knife
3 quart saucepan

Servings

Serves 4

Skill

Ingredients

28 ounces chicken broth, fat free (usually comes in a can or tetra pack)
3 cups water
⅓ cup green onions, sliced
½ teaspoon basil, dried
2 cloves garlic, finely chopped
8 ounces skinless, boneless chicken breast
8 ounces cheese tortellini
1 cup spinach, chopped
1 cup sugarsnap peas, sliced

Method

Remove any remaining skin or fat from the chicken breast. If your chicken breast is not exactly 8 ounces don't worry about it. A little more or less won't make any difference. Cut the chicken breast into bite-size chunks and set aside.

In 3 quart saucepan, mix together the broth, water, green onions, basil and garlic.

Note: If you are using bottled, already chopped garlic, used about 1 teaspoon.

Over medium-high heat, bring the broth mixture to a boil and add the chicken and tortellini.

Reduce the heat to medium and simmer for about 4 minutes.

Add the spinach and peas then continue to simmer for about 5 minutes, stirring occasionally. The tortellini should be tender and the chicken should be fully cooked, (no longer pink in the center).

Note: You are starting with broth so there should be no need to add any bouillon but if you taste it and decide you want a stronger flavour just add a chicken OXO cube.

Serve immediately.

PRESENTATION

If you like, you can add freshly ground pepper to taste.

Put the soup bowl on a dinner plate and add a few whole wheat crackers or slices of melba toast around the edge of the bowl.

MAIN DISHES OR ENTRÉES

We are going to start this section with some basic cooking tips for meat and vegetables. Recipes are great for special meals and for inspiration to try something different but mostly you just need the everyday basics.

In the second part you will find individual recipes that you can use to replace some of the basics to add more variety to your repertoire.

MEAT, VEGETABLE, STARCH

In North America the word entrée has come to mean the main dish but elsewhere it means the dish before the main meal.

For all of you that say you don't know how to cook it's time to pull back the curtain and reveal the secrets of the world's cooks.

No matter how many cookbooks you buy and how many fancy meals you will cook, the majority of your main meals will, most likely, be some variation of meat, starch, vegetable.

With that in mind we thought we would bring together a few thoughts on cooking these various components. This is one of those pick one from each of columns A, B and C things. You could make a few poor choices but for the most part you can put your meals together this way and end up with tasty, nutritious but otherwise uninspiring meals.

Nobody ever has to say they can't cook because the following couple of pages contain all you need to know to get by. This is just as easy as defrosting a frozen dinner or opening a can - but a whole lot better tasting and better for you.

The recipes in most cookbooks are just interesting and different ways to prepare one of these three things and they rarely concern themselves with the complete meal. It is up to you to select the dishes that go together. We suggest you start with basic preparation then substitute one of the more interesting variations for one of the three. In other words you might, for example, serve a basic pork chop with steamed broccoli and feta and lemon potatoes, which is the next recipe in this book.

DISCLAIMER
The following instructions are very general and should not be considered recipes. We include this section as a simple guide to the possibilities of day to day cooking. Basic cooking is not hard and can be successfully accomplished by anyone.

FRIED MEATS

Steaks, chops, sausages, ground meat, breaded (schnitzel), chicken

METHOD

Many meats can be cooked by simply placing them in a frying pan over medium heat (350°F) for about 20 minutes. Obviously you have to turn them over and cooking times will vary with the type of meat and the thickness of the cut.

ROAST MEATS

Certain cuts of beef, pork, lamb, chicken and turkey can all be roasted.

METHOD

Basically roasting means you put the meat in a pan which you put in an oven. The oven is generally set between 325°F and 375°F and most roasts take 20 - 30 minutes per pound. We strongly suggest you use a meat thermometer which you insert into the meat and read on the scale when your meat is ready.

GREEN VEGETABLES

Cabbage, broccoli, cauliflower, green beans, peas, spinach, zucchini

METHOD

The most basic way to cook green vegetables is to either boil or steam them. If you boil them then much of the goodness they contain will be thrown away with the cooking water.

Steaming is a better option and is just as quick. All you need is a steaming insert for a saucepan that you can get from any supermarket or kitchen store. The metal or plastic insert sits on the bottom of the pan and supports the vegetables above the water.

Steam your green vegetables for 10 - 15 minutes. Just use a fork to check if they are done. Don't overcook.

ROOT VEGETABLES

Potatoes, yams, carrots, parsnips, rutabagas

Method

Root vegetables can also be steamed although they may take a little longer than green vegetables. You can cook them all together in one pot by putting you root vegetables in 5 minutes ahead of the green vegetables.

You can also fry and roast root vegetables. A little butter, olive or coconut oil in a frying pan is all you need. Just stir occasionally to stop them from burning.

Oven roasting can also be done with very little oil. Just coat root vegetable pieces in coconut oil and put them in a shallow baking pan. 20 minutes at 400°F should be enough but turn the pieces after 10 minutes and check often until they are done.

Pasta & Grains

Pasta, rice, quinoa, couscous, bulgar wheat

Method

There are many ways to cook pasta and grains but the easiest is to boil them. Pasta such as spaghetti or macaroni is boiled in lightly salted water for about 10 minutes, then the water is drained.

Grains absorb the water they are cooked in so it is critical that you get the amount of water right. You may need up to twice as much water as grain but read the package directions for specific directions.

FETA AND LEMON POTATOES

SAFETY

This recipe calls for a very hot oven (450°F). At this temperature you might feel the heat of the baking dish even through your oven mitts. If the mitts are torn or not good quality you could even burn yourself.

EQUIPMENT YOU NEED

    Chef's knife
    Cutting board
    Measuring cup
    Large bowl
    9 x 13 inch baking dish

SERVINGS

    Serves 6

SKILL

    Zesting a lemon

INGREDIENTS

    4 large russet potatoes
    ¼ cup lemon juice
    1 tablespoon olive oil
    1½ tablespoons oregano
    2 teaspoons lemon zest*
    3 cloves garlic, finely chopped
    2 teaspoons salt
    1 cup water, boiling
    ⅔ cup feta cheese, crumbled
    * zest is grated skin (the lemon, not yours)

METHOD

Pre-heat the oven to 450°F.

Liberally grease a 9 inch x 13 inch baking dish. Use a non-stick cooking spray or butter.

Scrub the potatoes well (do not peel) and then slice, crosswise into ½ inch thick rounds.

In a large bowl, combine the potato slices, lemon juice, olive oil, oregano, lemon zest, garlic and salt. Toss well.

Pour the 1 cup of boiling water into the baking dish then layer the coated potato slices evenly in the water.

Bake uncovered at 450°F. for about 30 minutes or until most of the water has evaporated and the potatoes are fork-tender.

Evenly sprinkle the crumbled feta cheese over the top and continue to bake for another 15 minutes, until golden brown.

Remove from the oven and cool on a wire rack for a few minutes before serving.

PRESENTATION

Place the meat on the plate in the 6 o'clock position where it is easiest to cut, the potatoes at 2 o'clock and the green vegetable at 10 o'clock.

Spicy Oven Fries

Safety

Another very hot oven so heed the warning in the previous recipe.

Equipment You Need

Large bowl
Large baking sheet

Servings

Serves 2

Skill

Cutting uniform pieces of an ingredient.

Ingredients

2 large baking potatoes, preferably russet
1 tablespoon olive oil
1 tablespoon taco seasoning mix

Method

Pre-heat the oven to 450°F.

Coat a baking sheet with non-stick cooking spray.

Scrub the potatoes (do not peel) and cut, lengthwise, into wedges. Each potato should make 6-8 wedges. Pat the wedges dry with a paper towel.

Place the potatoes in a large bowl and sprinkle with the taco seasoning. Toss well to coat the wedges.

Drizzle the olive oil over the potatoes and toss again, making sure the wedges are well coated.

Arrange the potatoes in a single layer on the baking sheet.

Bake at 450°F. for 35-40 minutes or until the potatoes are slightly crisp and can be easily pierced with a fork.

Easy clean-up tip: Line the baking sheet with aluminum foil and spray that with cooking spray before putting the potatoes on it. That way you can just throw the foil away when your done and the baking sheet will be easy to wash.

PRESENTATION

Bring to the table in a wicker basket lined with parchment paper.

TWICE BAKED POTATOES

SAFETY

You are preparing very hot potatoes. Use your oven mitts or a folded paper towel to hold them.

EQUIPMENT YOU NEED

Cutting board
Chef's knife

SERVINGS

Serves 8

SKILL

Scooping out the cooked potato without breaking the skins.

INGREDIENTS

4 large baking potatoes
1 cup shredded cheddar cheese, divided
¾ cup sour cream
2 slices cooked bacon, crumbled
4 green onions, thinly sliced
1 teaspoon sea salt
½ teaspoon black pepper
1 clove garlic, finely chopped (or ready chopped and prepared in a jar)

METHOD

Pre-heat the oven to 400°F.

Wash, scrub and dry the potatoes. Pierce them with a fork in several places.

Place the potatoes directly on the middle oven rack and bake at 400°F for 45 minutes to one hour. They should give slightly when squeezed if they are done. (Be sure to use oven mitts when you squeeze them.)

Reduce the oven temperature to 350°F. Remove the potatoes from the oven and transfer them to a cutting board. Cut them in half lengthwise.

Carefully scoop out the potato flesh being sure to leave enough in the shells so the skins are still firm and not damaged. Place the scooped out portion in a large mixing bowl.

To the potato filling in the mixing bowl add ½ cup of the shredded cheddar cheese, the sour cream, crumbled bacon, sliced green onions, garlic, salt and pepper. Mix well. The mixture will be very thick.

Place the potato skins on a baking sheet and carefully spoon the mixture into each potato half.

Sprinkle the remaining ½ cup of shredded cheese evenly over the potatoes.

Bake at 350°F for about 30 minutes or until the cheese has started bubbling.

Remove from the oven and allow to them to cool slightly on a wire rack.

PRESENTATION

Bring them to the table on a long narrow serving platter and supply tongs so your guests can transfer them to their plates. A few sprigs of fresh parsley helps to dress up the plate.

Honey Glazed Carrots

Safety

Baby carrots just need washing so you don't even need to scrape the skins.

Equipment You Need

Medium saucepan
Wooden spoon
Serving dish

Servings

Serves 4 to 6

Skill

Honey, in any recipe, can burn very quickly. You need to keep things moving to be sure it doesn't burn.

Ingredients

1 pound baby carrots, washed
1 teaspoon table salt
2 tablespoons butter
2 tablespoons honey
1 tablespoon lemon juice
Black pepper, freshly ground
Sea salt, freshly ground

Method

To a medium saucepan, add the carrots, salt and sufficient water to cover the baby carrots. Bring the water to a boil and cook until the carrots are fork tender - about 5 or 6 minutes. Don't overcook.

Drain the carrots and return them to the saucepan. Add the butter, honey and lemon juice at the same time.

Note: if you'd like your glazed carrots to be sweet and hot, add a couple of dashes of Tabasco sauce to the pan as well.

Cook over medium heat, tossing the carrots so they get well glazed. This should take 2 or 3 minutes.

Season with salt and pepper and serve.

PRESENTATION

Bring to the table in a serving dish with a serving spoon and allow your guests to help themselves.

LEMON AND GARLIC BROCCOLI

SAFETY

Hot steam can scald just as easily as hot water.

EQUIPMENT YOU NEED

Small bowl or measuring cup
Steamer

SERVINGS

Serves 6

SKILL

Steaming vegetables

INGREDIENTS

2 heads broccoli, cut into spears
Water, for steaming
2 tablespoons olive oil
1 tablespoon lemon juice
2 garlic cloves, finely minced
1 teaspoon red pepper flakes, optional
1 teaspoon salt, or to taste

METHOD

In a stove-top or electric steamer, steam the broccoli for ten minutes. You can also use a steamer insert for your saucepan.

While the broccoli is steaming, mix together the olive oil, lemon juice, minced garlic, salt and red pepper flakes (if using).

Carefully remove the cooked broccoli from the steamer and transfer to a pre-warmed bowl or serving dish.

Pour the lemon garlic mixture over the broccoli and toss well to coat the broccoli.

Serve immediately.

PRESENTATION

Bring to the table in a serving dish with a serving spoon and allow your guests to help themselves.

Baked Chicken Breast

Safety

Raw chicken should always be handled with care as most of it contains Campylobacter and Salmonella bacteria. This is easily killed by proper cooking but be sure to thoroughly clean any surface that was in contact with the raw chicken to avoid the possibility of cross contamination with other foods.

Equipment You Need

9 inch x 13 inch glass baking dish
Small bowl or measuring cup
Serving platter

Servings

Serves 4

Skill

Applying a seasoning rub

Ingredients

4 chicken breasts, with bone and skin
¼ cup olive oil
1 teaspoon sea salt
½ teaspoon black pepper
½ teaspoon paprika
½ teaspoon garlic powder

Method

Pre-heat the oven to 350°F.

Coat a 9 inch x 13 inch glass baking dish with non-stick cooking spray. Set aside.

Thoroughly rinse and dry the chicken breasts. Set aside.

In a small bowl, mix together the salt, pepper, paprika and garlic powder.

Using a kitchen brush or your fingers, brush the olive oil on the chicken breasts being sure to coat them completely with a thin layer of the oil.

Sprinkle each breast with the spice mixture then rub the mixture in each breast well, using up all of the spice mixture.

Arrange the chicken breasts, skin side down, on the baking dish.

Bake at 350°F for 30 minutes, then turn the chicken breasts over so they are skin side up and bake for another 30 minutes.

Remove from oven and allow to cool slightly on a wire rack before serving.

PRESENTATION

You could bring this dish to the table on a large serving platter surrounded by vegetables or alternatively on a bed of rice.

Slow Cooker Salsa Chicken

Safety

As we explained in the previous recipe you must handle raw chicken with great care. Any surface that was in contact with the raw chicken must be thoroughly washed to avoid cross contamination.

Equipment You Need

Chef's knife
Cutting board
Measuring cup
Slow cooker

Servings

Serves 8

Skill

Using a slow cooker

Ingredients

2 stalks celery, sliced
4 large chicken breasts, boneless and skinless
2 tablespoons taco seasoning mix
1 cup salsa, medium or hot
1 can cream of chicken soup
1 red pepper, sliced
1 cup mushrooms, sliced
2 cups brown rice, cooked
½ cup sour cream
4 green onions, sliced

Method

Evenly distribute the sliced celery on the bottom of the slow cooker.

Cut each chicken breast in half and coat with the taco seasoning. Rub the seasoning into the chicken. Then place the chicken on top of the celery.

In a large measuring cup, mix the condensed cream of chicken soup and the salsa together. Gently pour the mixture over the chicken.

Set the slow cooker on low and cook for 6 to 8 hours. During the last hour of cooking add the diced red pepper and the sliced mushrooms.

Place each chicken breast on a pre-warmed plate along with ¼ cup of the cooked rice.

Spoon the sauce and celery from the slow cooker over the chicken and the rice.

PRESENTATION

Some slow cooker dishes are designed to be brought to the table otherwise you will need to transfer the contents to a serving dish.

Place a dollop of sour cream on top of the sauce and sprinkle ¼ of the sliced green onions on top of that.

EASY LATIN-STYLE RICE AND BEANS

SAFETY

Large frying pans full of food can get very heavy. You may need to hold the handle with two hands to stop the frying pan from tipping. Better to bring your plates to the pan and use a serving spoon to remove the mixture.

EQUIPMENT YOU NEED

Large frying pan or skillet

SERVINGS

Serves 4

SKILL

Adjusting seasonings to taste - particularly hot, spicy ones

INGREDIENTS

1 tablespoon olive oil
1 onion, finely chopped
1 tablespoon garlic, minced
1 red bell pepper, thinly sliced .
2 cups black beans, cooked .
¼ cup white vinegar
5-10 dashes Tabasco sauce
¼ cup fresh cilantro, chopped •
3 cups long grain rice, cooked
sea salt, freshly ground
black pepper, freshly ground

METHOD

Note: This recipe calls for cooked black beans and cooked rice which you will need to prepare first.

In a large skillet, heat the olive oil over medium-high heat. Add the onions and cook, stirring occasionally, for 5-7 minutes or until the onions are translucent.

Add the garlic and red peppers and cook for another 2-3 minutes.

Add the black beans, vinegar and Tobasco sauce and bring the mixture to a boil.

Add the chopped cilantro and cooked rice. Mix well and season to taste with freshly ground salt and pepper.

PRESENTATION

Serve with a side salad and some extra hot sauce for a great, meatless meal.

CHICKEN AND CASHEW STIR FRY

SAFETY

This is another raw chicken recipe which means you need to be extra careful with kitchen hygiene. Never serve undercooked chicken and always wash knives and cutting boards with hot soapy water.

EQUIPMENT YOU NEED

Medium bowl
Measuring cup
Stove top or electric wok*

SERVINGS

Serves 4

SKILL

Learn to make a good stir fry and you have the basis for hundreds of different original meals. You can use all kinds of different fresh vegetables - just use your imagination.

INGREDIENTS

2 chicken breasts, boneless and skinless
2 tablespoons soy sauce
1 tablespoon fresh ginger, grated
3 cloves garlic, minced
1 teaspoon honey
¾ cup chicken broth
4 teaspoons cornstarch
3 tablespoons peanut oil
2 cups broccoli, chopped
1 red bell pepper, thinly sliced
1 onion, thinly sliced
1 cup sugar snap peas
1 cup mushrooms, sliced
½ cup cashew halves

METHOD

Cut the chicken breast into one-inch strips.

In a medium bowl, mix together the soy sauce, honey, garlic and ginger. Add the chicken strips and toss well. Set aside.

In a one-cup measuring cup, whisk together the chicken broth and cornstarch. Set aside.

In a wok or deep skillet, heat 2 tablespoons of the peanut oil over medium-high heat.

Add the sliced onion, chopped broccoli and sliced red pepper to the hot oil and stir fry for 5-6 minutes.

Add the other tablespoon of peanut oil. Then add the chicken and soy sauce mixture and stir fry for another 6-7 minutes or until the chicken is fully cooked an no longer pink.

Add the chicken broth and cornstarch mixture. (Be sure to stir the mixture well before adding so you don't get any lumps)

Add the sliced mushrooms and sugar snaps peas and cook for 2-3 minutes or until the mixture has thickened.

Stir in the cashews and serve over hot rice or noodles.

STIR FRYING

The steep sides of a wok prevent a large quantity of food being in contact with the heat at any one time. Therefore, you usually use a slightly higher temperature than normal and keep the food moving so it all has a chance to contact the heat at the bottom of the pan.

PRESENTATION

You have several options for presenting the rice and vegetables. Besides putting the vegetables on top of the rice you can lay them beside each other or have one encircle the other.

For this recipe you could also cook the chicken mixture separately from the vegetables and serve them on separate areas of the plate.

* a wok is like a frying pan but it has very high sides at a steep angle.

QUICK AND EASY BEEF STROGANOFF

SAFETY

The easiest, safest way to drain any boiled food is to use a colander.

EQUIPMENT YOU NEED

Large frying pan or skillet
Colander

SERVINGS

Serves 6

SKILL

Recipes will often tell you to follow package directions which are in addition to the instructions in the recipe.

INGREDIENTS

1½ pounds lean ground beef
½ cup onion, chopped
1 teaspoon salt
½ teaspoon black pepper
3 tablespoons flour
½ cup beef broth
1 cup mushrooms, sliced
1 can cream of mushroom soup, undiluted
1 cup sour cream
3 cups egg noodles, cooked per package instructions

METHOD

In a large skillet, over medium-high heat, brown the ground beef. Drain the ground beef and set aside.

In the slight amount of fat remaining in the skillet, after ground beef has been drained, cook the chopped onions over medium heat until translucent.

Return the ground beef to the skillet and add the salt, pepper and flour. Still well.

Slowly stir in the beef broth, stirring constantly to make sure the flour and beef broth get well mixed.

Add the sliced mushrooms and cook for 2-3 minutes. Then add the cream of mushroom soup and the sour cream and cook until everything is warmed through. The mixtures should start to bubble.

Remove from heat and serve over cooked egg noddles.

PRESENTATION

A small side salad would go nicely with this dish, as would some garlic bread.

PASTA

You can use individual servings of different kinds of pasta to replace potatoes in your basic meals or you can make all kinds of pasta based recipes.

We've included a couple of easy pasta recipes to get you started but there are so many great things you can make we will have to write a whole book about it.

Spaghetti With Spicy Baked Meatballs

Boiling spaghetti and heating a can or jar of sauce is quite possibly the easiest meal you can make. This is a Friday night meal when you have to decide between it and ordering a pizza.

But it doesn't have to be that way, you can make a spaghetti meal into an event. You can make both the spaghetti and the sauce from scratch and get something totally different from the package and jar taste.

We recommend you try making everything from scratch at least once but for this book we want to concentrate on something between the two extremes. We will use fresh pasta that you can buy from most supermarkets and ready-made sauce which we are going to spice up a bit.

You can also buy ready made frozen meatballs but then you also get all the preservatives and other junk the food corporations add to our food. Best to make our own!

Safety

There are two areas of concern with this dish. Namely draining the spaghetti and taking the meatballs out of the oven. Please use a colander to drain the spaghetti and well fitting oven mitts when removing anything from the oven.

Equipment You Need

Spaghetti measuring tool - This is a plastic tool that has 4 holes of different sizes corresponding to different serving sizes. Just select the number of servings and measure the size of your spaghetti bundle. It only works with the dry rigid commercial spaghetti and not with fresh spaghetti.
Large saucepan
Colander
Oven broiler pan

SERVINGS

Serves 12

SKILL

Forming uniform meatballs

INGREDIENTS - MEATBALLS

1½ pounds lean ground beef - or ground turkey or a mixture of the two

2 teaspoons Worcestershire sauce

1 egg, beaten

½ cup oatmeal

¼ cup parmesan cheese, grated

2 garlic cloves, minced

1 teaspoon sea salt

½ teaspoon black pepper

½ teaspoon red pepper flakes, optional

INGREDIENTS - SPAGHETTI

1 pound spaghetti, preferably fresh, prepared according to package directions

INGREDIENTS - SAUCE

1 jar or can of pasta sauce

METHOD - MEATBALLS

Pre-heat your oven to 425°F.

Grease a broiler pan with a non-stick spray.

Note: we're going to use a broiler pan so that any excess grease will drip into the bottom of the broiler pan.

In a large bowl combine the ground beef, Worcestershire sauce, egg, oatmeal, parmesan cheese, garlic, salt, pepper and red pepper flakes (if using). Mix well.

Note: Mixing with your hands is probably the best way to make sure everything gets mixed together well. Just make sure you wash your hands well, before and after.

Form the meat mixture into balls about 1½ inches in diameter and place them on the greased grill pan.

Bake at 425°F for about 10-15 minutes. Cut one slightly to make sure it is no longer pink in the middle. Baking time will vary depending on the size of the meatballs.

Turn off the oven and let the meatballs stay warm while you prepare the spaghetti according to the package directions and heat the spaghetti sauce.

Note: You can add an onion to your meatballs but you will find they don't hold together very well. If you do add onion be sure to chop it very fine.

METHOD - SAUCE

If you are not making your sauce from scratch you must rely on the jar or canned sauces and they vary greatly in taste and quality. Even when you find one you like you may want to spice it up a bit. We like a thick sauce that sticks to the spaghetti and we like it spicy. Over the years we have tried many brands and have settled on Hunts Thick & Rich as our sauce of choice.

We cannot give you any specific directions since we don't know what you are starting with but a few additions you can try are garlic, Italian spice, Romano cheese, poultry seasoning (really), red pepper flakes. red and green bell peppers.

PRESENTATION

A spaghetti serving dish has a large diameter and is shallow (3 or 4 inches deep). A spaghetti serving spoon looks like a regular spoon with 3 or 4 'fingers' on either side.

For cutlery you need a fork and a dessert spoon. If you are right-handed hold the fork in your right hand, pick up some spaghetti and put the fork tines in the spoon as you twirl the fork and wrap the spaghetti around the fork. It takes a little practice but once you get the knack you will find it much easier than cutting the spaghetti into little bits.

SLOW COOKER PIZZA-STYLE PASTA

SAFETY

Draining fat from a hot frying pan can be difficult. Don't try to pour it off as you risk dropping the hot pan and the contents. Use a slotted spoon to scoop the ingredients from the pan leaving the grease behind.

EQUIPMENT YOU NEED

Frying pan or skillet
Slow cooker

SERVINGS

Serves 8

SKILL

Using a slow cooker

INGREDIENTS

2 pounds ground beef
10 ounce can tomato soup, undiluted
28 ounces pizza sauce
8 ounces pepperoni, chopped
8 ounces rigatoni pasta
8 ounces mozzarella cheese, shredded

METHOD

In a large skillet, over medium-high heat, brown the ground beef and drain off the fat.

Combine the ground beef, tomato soup, pizza sauce and pepperoni in a slow cooker and mix well.

Cover and set slow cooker to low. Cook for 4 hours.

Approximately ½ hour before you are ready to serve this dish, stir in the uncooked rigatoni and replace the lid.

PRESENTATION

When you are ready to serve, you can either stir in the shredded Mozzarella cheese or use it to sprinkle on top of each dish.

Fiesta Chicken and Penne

Safety

Food graters don't look very dangerous but they can give you a nasty cut if you're not careful. Watch out when you're down to the small pieces.

Equipment You Need

Large saucepan
Large bowl
Colander

Servings

Serves 6

Skill

Shredding or grating cheese
Tip: Softer cheeses are easier to grate if you freeze them

Ingredients

16 ounces penne pasta
2 cups cooked chicken, cubed
1¼ cups salsa
2 ounces cheddar cheese, shredded
½ cup milk
¼ teaspoon salt

Method

Cook the dry penne pasta according to the package directions.

While the penne is cooking, in a large bowl, combine the cooked chicken, salsa, milk, salt and shredded cheese.

Drain the pasta and return it to the saucepan.

Stir in the chicken mixture and toss well, making sure the pasta gets well coated.

Cook over medium heat until everything is heated through - about 8-10 minutes.

PRESENTATION

Serve with a small side salad and a little grated cheese on the top.

DESSERTS

Fresh fruit is always a healthy dessert choice and there are numerous varieties to choose from. But sometimes you want something more and although you know you sugar is bad for you, having it once in a while is OK.

We don't claim these recipes are particularly healthy but they do taste wonderful.

CREAMY BAKED RICE PUDDING

Rice pudding is one of the easiest desserts to make and is liked by most people. You can serve it hot or cold and dress it up with fruit, jam or cream.

If you use rice as a vegetable you use long grain rice, for dessert use short grain rice.

SAFETY

Before you remove any item from a hot oven be sure you have planned what to do with it. If you plan to put it on the counter make sure there is a heat proof surface available - often a wooden cutting board is a good choice.

Also make sure you have good quality, well fitting oven mitts.

EQUIPMENT YOU NEED

Measuring cup
Wooden spoon
3 quart baking dish with optional lid

SERVINGS

Serves 10

SKILL

Rice absorbs a lot of liquid. When you prepare the ingredients you may think there is way too much milk but just wait and you will see it all gets sucked up. Use too much rice and you will end up with a solid lump.

INGREDIENTS

1 cup short grain white rice, uncooked
4 cups milk
½ cup white sugar
1 teaspoon vanilla extract
½ teaspoon ground nutmeg
⅓ cup raisins, optional

Method

Pre-heat the oven to 275°F.

In a well-greased, 3 quart baking dish (preferably one with a lid), combine all the ingredients with the exception of the raisins (if using). Mix well.

You can use any type of milk including UHT and canned milk but your choice will change the taste.

Bake at 275°F. for 3 hours or until the desired consistency is reached. Stir once after first hour. If using raisins, stir them in for the last hour of cooking.

Note: You can bake the rice pudding either covered or uncovered. If you leave it uncovered a skin will form on the top which many people like. If you cover it, then the skin should not form.

Presentation

Suggestion: Serve in a glass goblet with a short stem and top with whipped cream and a maraschino cherry.

Your Choice Pudding Pie

This is possibly the easiest recipe in the book. It is one of those things you can easily whip up for dessert when company arrives unexpectedly. Just keep the ingredients around all the time and you'll never be caught short.

Safety

The only possible safety concern here is with the cooked pudding which will stick to you and burn if you spill any.

Equipment You Need

Saucepan for cooked pudding
Bowl or measuring cup for instant pudding

Servings

Serves 6 - 8

Skill

Being prepared for unexpected company

Ingredients

Cooked or instant pudding - chocolate, vanilla, banana, lemon, pistachio
8 inch graham cracker or pastry pie shell
See below for add-in and garnish suggestions

Method

Prepare the pudding per the package directions.

Note: You can use either instant or cooked pudding but we believe the cooked has a better texture

Pour the pudding into the pie shell and chill for at least an hour before serving.

Suggestions for add-ins.

Add-ins should be placed on the pie shell before pouring the pudding on top.

Sliced bananas
Sliced pears
Sliced peaches
Sliced Apricots
Whole or sliced strawberries
Jam of your choice

Suggestions for garnishes

whipped cream
chocolate chips or sprinkles
fresh fruit
chopped nuts
shredded coconut

PRESENTATION

Store bought pie shells usually come in a foil pie plate so you will want to prepare individual servings for your guests.

Velvet Jello™ on a Hill

Everybody loves Jello and this twist makes an attractive presentation and a new taste.

Safety

The steam from boiling water can burn you - just be careful.

Equipment You Need

Measuring cup
Stirring spoon
6 "Old Fashioned" glasses. These are the tumblers that are about 3 inches tall. An Old Fashioned is an alcoholic drink that is served in this type of glass.

Servings

Serves 6

Skill

Learn to be creative in your presentation. The taste may be the same but an attractive presentation makes the experience better.
You can add all kinds of fruit to Jello except fresh pineapple. If you use fresh pineapple your Jello will not set.

Ingredients

package of Jello or other brand of gelatin
canned milk

Method

Make as per package directions but replace the cold water with canned milk.

Pour an equal amount into each glass.

Stand one edge of each glass on something about ½ inch high so that the liquid will set at an angle.

PRESENTATION

There are lots of fun things you can do with Jello. Look in kitchen stores for molds in interesting shapes. Try pouring the liquid over cake so that it soaks in before it sets.

Slow Cooker Raisin Bread Pudding

Safety

In this recipe you will be adding boiling water to the ingredients. Be very careful with the boiling water. Both the steam and the water can give you a nasty burn.

Equipment You Need

Slow cooker
Measuring cup
Measuring spoons

Servings

Serves 8

Skill

Gently and slowly pouring liquid ingredients over solid ingredients to achieve a uniform consistency.

Ingredients

6 cups raisin bread, cubed
½ cup raisins
6 eggs
1 cup instant dry milk powder
2 teaspoon vanilla
½ teaspoon cinnamon
1 cup brown sugar
¼ teaspoon salt
1½ cups boiling water

Method

Coat the inside of your slow cooker with non-stick cooking spray.

Evenly distribute the bread cubes in the slow cooker and sprinkle with the raisins.

In a large measuring cup, combine the remaining ingredients and mix well.

Gently pour the liquid mixture over the bread cubes and raisins.

Cover and set slow cooker to high. Cook for about 3 hours or until a toothpick inserted in the center comes out clean.

PRESENTATION

Serve warm and garnish with custard, whipped cream or maple syrup.

Cherry Walnut Bread Pudding With Custard

This is a twist on a traditional English dessert and traditionally is served with Birds Custard. Fortunately Birds Custard has become so popular that it is available around the world and you can most likely find it at your local supermarket.

SAFETY

Observe all the usual safety precautions of using a hot oven particularly well fitting, quality oven mitts.

EQUIPMENT YOU NEED

Medium size mixing bowl
Fork
6 ramekins. A ramekin is a small porcelain or stoneware dish for serving an individual portion that can also go in the oven.

SERVINGS

Serves 6

SKILL

Changing the presentation by cooking as individual servings.

INGREDIENTS

4 cups bread
½ cup sugar (white or brown)
3 eggs
2 cups whole milk
¼ cup butter
½ cup dried cherries
½ cup walnut halves
2 teaspoons vanilla
1 teaspoon cinnamon
¼ teaspoon allspice

¼ teaspoon salt

grated nutmeg (optional)

METHOD

Preheat your oven to 350°F

Tear the bread into ½ inch pieces. You can use store bought "squeezable" bread if that is all you have but home made Italian bread would be better. Raisin bread is another good choice.

In a medium bowl beat the eggs with a fork.

Add the sugar, melted butter and spices. Then stir until the sugar is dissolved.

Add the bread and break up the pieces with your fork.

Add the milk and whisk the mixture with a fork until fairly smooth.

Pour about ⅔ cup of the mixture into each ramekin.

Add an equal amount of cherries and walnuts to each ramekin. If you add the cherries and walnuts to the mixture in the bowl they may not get evenly distributed into the ramekins.

Bake at 350°F for 35-40 minutes. You know it's done when the top no longer looks wet and a toothpick inserted in the middle comes out clean.

Sprinkle the top with grated nutmeg if you like.

We prefer our bread pudding cold so we make it ahead and put it in the refrigerator. If you like yours warm just pop the raw mixture into the oven when you sit down for your main course.

PRESENTATION

As we said in the introduction this is traditionally served with Birds Custard that you make using the package directions but you could top with ice cream, whipped cream, jam, marshmallow - just use your imagination.

WALNUT-STUFFED BAKED APPLES

SAFETY

Coring apples is pretty easy if you have an apple corer. If you don't, you're going to need to use a knife. You need to be very careful and should have the help of an adult if you're using a knife to core the apples.

EQUIPMENT YOU NEED

Apple corer
Oven proof baking dish
Measuring cups
Measuring spoons

SERVINGS

Serves 4

SKILL

Coring an apple

INGREDIENTS

4 large baking apples
¼ cup brown sugar, packed
1 teaspoon cinnamon
¼ cup walnuts, chopped
¼ cup raisins
1 tablespoon butter
2 cups vanilla ice cream

METHOD

Pre-heat oven to 375°F.

Wash the apples well and remove the cores, making the opening about ¾ inch wide. This is easiest to do with an apple corer. If you don't have one, you can use a paring knife, but you'll need to be very, very careful. Make sure you have all of the core and the seeds out.

Spray an 8 inch square glass baking dish with non-stick cooking spray and arrange the cored apples in the dish. Cut a little off the bottom of the apples if you need to to make them stand up properly.

In a small bowl, mix the sugar, cinnamon, raisins and walnuts together.

Stuff each apple with ¼ of this mixture and put a ¼ tablespoon of butter on top of each one.

Bake at 375°F. for 30-40 minutes. The apples should be tender but not mushy.

Remove from oven and allow to cool on a wire rack for about 5-10 minutes.

PRESENTATION
Serve warm with a scoop of vanilla ice cream on the side.

BEVERAGES

Tap water is your best beverage choice. If you want a little flavour you can squeeze a piece of orange, lemon or lime into the water.

For hot drinks herbal teas are available in a dizzying variety of flavours. Regular tea and coffee are OK in limited quantities but try to avoid soda's and pop that are loaded with sugar and caffeine.

Unfortunately, thanks to the huge food corporation, even milk is no longer a healthy choice as it contains all kinds of chemicals and genetically engineered components.

But if you want an occasional milkshake or smoothie you can either travel to Europe, where they have much stricter food laws, or take your chances with the chemicals.

Thick Milkshake

Safety

Not exactly a safety issue but you must be sure your blender lid is securely in place. You should also keep one hand on the lid while blending as the pressure of the moving ingredients can push the lid off the glass container.

Equipment You Need

Electric Blender
Ice cream scoop
Tall glass

Servings

Serves 1

Skill

Using a blender

Ingredients

3 scoops ice cream, flavor of your choice
½ cup milk
3 tablespoons syrup, flavor of your choice, optional

Method

Combine all the ingredients in an electric blender and blend until smooth.

Pour into a tall glass and serve with a straw.

Presentation

Garnish if desired. For example, a strawberry on the side of the glass for a strawberry shake or some chocolate sprinkles for a chocolate shake.

Fruit Smoothies

Safety

Read the warning in the previous milkshake recipe about the lid popping off the blender. Also be careful when cutting a frozen banana. Use a cutting board and the rocking chef knife technique.

Equipment You Need

Electric blender
Chef's knife
Cutting board
2 tall glasses

Servings

Serves 2

Skill

Pulsing a blender.

Ingredients

Frozen banana, peeled and sliced
2 cups frozen strawberries, raspberries, blueberries, blackberries, or any combination
1 cup milk
½ cup plain yogurt
½ cup orange or pineapple juice
2 tablespoons honey

Method

Place all ingredients in an electric blender and pulse until the large lumps of fruit are chopped then blend on high until smooth.

Pulsing - Some blenders have a pulse setting. If not you just quickly turn the blender on and off to chop the frozen fruit.

Pour into glasses and serve.

PRESENTATION

Garnish, if desired, with whole strawberry, a pineapple chunk on the side of the glass. Or sprinkle a few berries on the top.

BAKING

You can treat most recipes as suggestions and modify ingredients and quantities based on your own experience but baking is different. The baking recipes involve a lot of kitchen chemistry that you should only change if you really know what you are doing.

Sure you can substitute chunks of apple for raisins in a muffin recipe but don't mess with things like flour, eggs, salt and baking powder.

Magic Cookie Dough

This recipe should create a total of four dozen cookies. For this batch we will make four different kinds from a single batch of dough - Rum Raisin, Peanut Butter, Pecan Sandies and Sandwich Sugar Cookies (with Strawberry Jam in the middle).

Safety

You may be tempted to try the cookie dough as you make these but it's not a good idea to eat food containing raw eggs. Raw eggs may contain a bacteria that causes food poisoning.

Equipment You Need

Large mixing bowl
Measuring cups
Measuring spoons
Baking sheet

Servings

4 dozen cookies

Skill

Working with cookie dough

Basic Dough Ingredients

3½ - 4 cups all purpose flour
1 teaspoon baking powder
½ teaspoon salt
1 cup butter or margarine
1½ cups sugar
2 eggs
1½ teaspoons vanilla

Rum Raisin Ingredients

¼ cup raisins
¼ cup rum, preferably dark

Peanut Butter Ingredients

⅓ cup peanut butter, chunky or smooth depending on your preference

Pecan Sandies Ingredients

¼ cup pecans, chopped to the consistency of a coarse meal

Sandwich Sugar Cookies Ingredients

Sugar for dusting the cookie tops
Jam of your choice for the filling

Method

Cream the butter or margarine (see glossary) and gradually add the sugar.

Add the eggs and blend thoroughly.

Add the vanilla.

Combine the flour, baking powder and salt and mix thoroughly.

Add the dry ingredients to the butter mixture gradually and mix after each addition. We like to do the final mixing with our hands. If you find that the dough is sticking to your hands you can add up to another ½ cup of flour.

When the desired consistency has been achieved, divide the dough into four equal pieces (if you plan to make four different types of cookies). We weighed the dough to make it easier to divide. We found this recipe made about 40 ounces of dough, so we divided it into 10 ounce pieces.

For Rum Raisin Cookies

Soak the raisins in rum for two or three hours.

Add the raisins and any remaining rum to ¼ of the basic dough recipe and mix well. Add a little more flour if you need to soak up any extra rum.

Cover and refrigerate for one hour.

For Peanut Butter Cookies

Add ⅓ cup of peanut butter to ¼ of the basic dough recipe and mix well.

Cover and refrigerate for one hour.

For Pecan Sandies

Add ¼ cup pecans, chopped to the consistency of a coarse meal, to ¼ of the basic dough and mix well.

Cover and refrigerate for one hour.

For Sandwich Sugar Cookies

Cover and refrigerate, for one hour, the remaining ¼ of the basic dough.

Forming And Baking The Cookies

Preheat the oven to 375°F.

Grease the cookie sheets. We usually use two large cookie sheets and we spray them with a non-stick spray.

Forming And Baking The Rum Raisin Cookies

Form dough into approximately 12 small balls by rolling between the palms of your hands.

Place each ball onto the greased cookie sheet and press down with the flat of your fingers.

Bake at 375°F for about 10 to 12 minutes. Bottoms will be brown and edges will just be starting to brown.

Transfer to a cooling rack and allow to cool.

Forming And Baking The Peanut Butter Cookies

Form dough into approximately 12 small balls by rolling between the palms of your hands.

Place each ball onto the greased cookie sheet and press down with the flat of your fingers, then use fork tines to make lines first one way and then at 90 degrees.

Bake at 375°F for about 10 to 12 minutes. Bottoms will be brown and edges will just be starting to brown.

Transfer to a cooling rack and allow to cool.

Forming And Baking The Pecan Sandies

Form dough into approximately 12 small balls by rolling between the palms of your hands.

Place each ball onto the greased cookie sheet and press down slightly with the back of a spoon.

Bake at 375°F for about 10 to 12 minutes. Bottoms will be brown and edges will just be starting to brown.

Transfer to a cooling rack and allow to cool.

Forming And Baking The Sandwich Sugar Cookies

Lightly flour a flat surface where you can roll out the dough.

Take a portion of the chilled dough and form into a thick disc.

Place it on the floured surface and sprinkle a bit more flour on the top.

Roll out as thin as possible.

Use a cookie cutter to cut out circles to be used for the bottom of the sandwich. For the tops, use the same size cookie cutter and use a much smaller one to create the hole in the center.

Carefully transfer the sugar cookies to the greased cookie sheet.

Sprinkle sugar on the "top" cookies only.

Bake at 375°F for about 6 to 8 minutes. Watch them carefully as they can brown very quickly.

Transfer to a cooling rack and allow to cool completely.

Spread a thin layer of jam on the bottom cookie and place a top cookie on the top the make the sandwich.

Other Variations:

You can, of course, add whatever you'd like. Just use the quantities specified in these recipes as a guide line. For example: to make chocolate chip cookies, just add ¼ cup chocolate chips to ¼ of the basic dough recipe. You get the idea!

Blueberry Muffins

Safety

400°F is a hot oven. Be careful reaching across the oven door and make sure you are wearing well fitting oven mitts.

Equipment You Need

Large mixing bowl
Measuring cups
Measuring spoons
Muffin pan

Servings

12 muffins

Skill

Distributing the batter evenly between each muffin.

Ingredients

1 cup all purpose flour
1 cup whole wheat flour
¾ cup sugar
3 teaspoons baking powder
¼ cup butter
1 egg, large
1 cup milk
2 cups blueberries, fresh or frozen

Method

Pre-heat oven to 400°F. and coat muffin tin with non-stick spray.

In a large bowl, mix together the flour, sugar and baking powder.

Using a pastry blender, cut the butter into the flour mixture until it resembles coarse oatmeal.

In a large measuring cup, beat the egg, then add the milk and mix well.

Add the milk and egg mixture to the dry ingredients and mix with a fork just until moist. The batter will be a bit lumpy.

Add the blueberries and mix only until the berries are well distributed through the batter.

Fill muffin tins about ¾ full.

Bake at 400°F. for 20-25 minutes or until muffin tops a slightly browned and a toothpick inserted in the center comes out clean.

Remove from oven and cool on a wire rack.

PRESENTATION
Serve warm from the oven with a pat of butter.

Basic Frosting Recipe

Safety

There had to be one recipe in the book that was safe.

Equipment You Need

Large mixing bowl
Electric mixer

Servings

1 two layer cake

Skill

Making and applying frosting

Ingredient

⅓ cup butter, softened
¼ teaspoon salt
1 teaspoon vanilla
1 pound confectioners sugar
3 tablespoons heavy cream, approximately
3 or 4 drops food coloring, optional
⅓ cup cocoa powder, optional

Method

In a large bowl, cream together the butter, salt and vanilla, using an electric mixer on low speed. Beat until light and fluffy.

Add 3 tablespoons of heavy whipping cream (35%) and beat until smooth.

Add food coloring of your choice, if desired and beat until the color is consistent throughout.

If you would like to make chocolate frosting, add ⅓ cup unsweetened cocoa powder and beat until well mixed.

Note: You may need to add more heavy cream to achieve the desired consistency. Only add 1 teaspoon of heavy cream at a time.

PRESENTATION

Spread the frosting on the top and sides of the cake using a frosting spatula. You can use a regular dinner knife but you will find the frosting spatula is easier and does a better job.

If you split the frosting into two batches before you add any food coloring you can make two different colors and get creative with swirls and other patterns.

Two Layer Sponge Cake With Strawberry Jam And Whipped Cream

Safety

All the usual warnings of working with a hot oven apply. Well fitting oven mitts and care when reaching across an open oven door.

Equipment You Need

Large mixing bowl
Electric mixer
Two 9 inch cake pans
Measuring cups
Measuring spoons
Cooling rack

Servings

Serves 12

Skill

Whipping cream and assembling and frosting a layer cake

Ingredients

2¼ cups all purpose flour
1½ cups sugar
1 tablespoon baking powder
1 teaspoon salt
½ cup butter, softened
1 cup milk, divided
1 teaspoon vanilla
2 eggs
¼ cup strawberry jam
1/2 pint container of 30% (or higher) whipping cream, whipped

METHOD

Spray two 9 inch round cake pans with non-stick cooking spray and dust with flour.

Note: the easiest way to dust a cake pan with flour is to sprinkle 1 or 2 tablespoons of flour into the pan and then shake and turn the pan to distribute the flour evenly. Shake out any excess flour.

Pre-heat the oven to 350°F.

In a large bowl, cream (see glossary) the butter and sugar together. Add ¾ cup milk, the vanilla and the eggs. Mix using a electric mixer on slow speed.

In a separate bowl or measuring cup, mix together the flour, salt and baking powder.

Using an electric mixer on slow speed, gradually add the flour mixture alternately with the remaining 1/4 cup of milk. Increase mixer speed to medium and beat for 2 minutes.

Pour equal amounts of the batter into each of the prepared cake pans.

Bake at 350°F for 25 minutes or until a toothpick inserted in the center of the cakes comes out clean.

Remove cakes from the oven and cool on a wire rack for 10 minutes. Remove cakes from cake pans and cool completely on wire rack.

Once both cakes are completely cool, place one layer on a cake plate. Spread the strawberry jam and whipped cream on the first layer and top with the second layer.

PRESENTATION

You can leave it plain or frost the top and sides of the layer cake using the previous recipe for a basic frosting.

Garnish, if desired, with some fresh strawberries and a few chocolate curls.

HOW TO WHIP CREAM

EQUIPMENT

Deep, narrow container
Electric mixer with whisk attachment

Method

Chill the container and whisk for ½ hour before you begin. Cream should be as cold as possible but not frozen.

You use a deep container because you want the cream to cover the blades of the whisk. You will need to securely hold the container while you are whipping.

Always start at the slowest speed and gradually increase the speed so you don't spray cream all over the kitchen. Keep whipping until peaks stand up but don't whip too much or you will get butter.

We like to add up to 2 tablespoons of sugar to ½ pint of cream but this is optional. We also like to add ¼ teaspoon of pure vanilla extract.

Basic Cupcake Recipe

Safety

We cannot emphasize enough how important well fitting oven mitts are when taking hot dishes from the oven.

Equipment You Need

Muffin pan
Mixing bowl
Measuring cups
Measuring spoons

Servings

Serves 12

Skill

Not overfilling the muffin cups to allow room for rising.

Ingredients

½ cup butter, softened
⅔ cup sugar
2 eggs
1 teaspoon vanilla
1 cup flour
1 teaspoon baking powder
½ teaspoon salt

Method

Pre-heat oven to 350°F

In a large bowl, cream the butter and sugar together. Add the vanilla and eggs and mix well.

In a separate 2 cup measuring cup, mixed together the flour, baking powder and salt.

Add the flour mixture to the egg mixture and mix well.

Coat muffin tins with non-stick cooking spray or line each muffin tin with paper muffin cups.

Fill each muffin tin about half full with the cupcake batter.

Bake at 350°F for 15 to 20 minutes or until a toothpick inserted in the certain of a cupcake comes out clean.

Remove from oven and allow to cool on a wire rack.

Here are some suggestions for add-ins to this basic recipe (add about 1/2 cup to the egg mixture before adding the flour mixture): chocolate chips, raisins, craisins, chopped nuts.

PRESENTATION

You can frost the cupcakes using a pre-made frosting of your choice or the basic frosting recipe in this book.

Zucchini Bread

Safety

For the last time in this book we want to caution you about wearing well fitting oven mitts and reaching across open oven doors.

Equipment You Need

Two 9 inch by 5 inch loaf pans
Grater
Measuring cups
Measuring spoons
Chef knife
Chopping board

Servings

Serves 24

Skill

There is nothing more satisfying than baking your own bread.

Ingredients

2 eggs, beaten
1 ⅓ cup sugar
2 teaspoons vanilla
3 cups zucchini, grated
⅔ cup unsweetened apple sauce
2 teaspoons baking soda
¼ teaspoon salt
3 cups all-purpose flour
½ teaspoon nutmeg
2 teaspoons cinnamon
1 cup walnuts, chopped, optional
1 cup raisins or craisins, optional

METHOD

Pre-heat oven to 350°F.

Coat two 9-inch by 5-inch loaf pans with non-stick cooking spray.

In a large bowl, mix together the sugar, eggs and vanilla. Mix in the grated zucchini and unsweetened apple sauce.

In a separate bowl, mix together the flour, baking soda, salt, cinnamon and nutmeg.

Slowly add the dry mixture to the zucchini mixture until everything is incorporated and the mixture is moist. Do not over mix.

Fold in the nuts and raisins (or craisins) if you've decided to use them.

Divide the batter equally between the two loaf pans.

Bake at 350°F. for about one hour. Start checking after about 45 minutes. A wooden toothpick inserted in the center of the loaf will come out clean when it is done.

Remove from oven and allow to cool on a wire rack.

Once the loaves have cooled, remove from loaf pans and slice.

This zucchini bread freezes well.

PRESENTATION

Warm zucchini bread is nice served with apple sauce.

APPENDIX

We've included a glossary and an international table of weights and measures that we hope you will find useful.

INTERNATIONAL MEASUREMENT EQUIVALENTS

This book uses standard US weights and measurements so I have included this chart so you can adjust the recipes to your local system. Equivalents are not exact but close enough for cooking.

DRY MEASURE

Dry measurements are not generally used in US recipes. Only fresh produce such as berries might be measured by the pint. If a US recipe calls for a Pint, Quart or Gallon it is referring to dry measurement which is not the same as liquid measurement.

1 pint, dry = 1.1636 pints, liquid

1 quart, dry = 1.1636 quarts, liquid

1 gallon, dry = 1.1636 gallons, liquid

LIQUID MEASURE

Under the US system not only liquids like milk and water use a liquid measurement but other ingredients such as flour, sugar, shortening, butter, and spices. Note the difference between a US and an Imperial gallon

1 teaspoon (tsp) = $\frac{1}{3}$ tablespoon (tbsp) = $\frac{1}{6}$ fluid ounce

1 tablespoon (tbsp) = 3 teaspoons (tsp) = $\frac{1}{2}$ fluid ounce = $\frac{1}{16}$ cup

1 fluid ounce = 6 teaspoons (tsp) = 2 tablespoons (tbsp) = $\frac{1}{8}$ cup

1 cup = 48 teaspoons = 16 tablespoons (tbsp) = 8 fluid ounces = 1 cup = 236 millilitre (ml)

1 pint = 96 teaspoons (tsp) = 32 tablespoons (tbsp) = 16 fluid ounces = 2 cups = 473 millilitre (ml)

1 quart = 192 teaspoons (tsp) = 64 tablespoons (tbsp) = 32 fluid ounces = 4 cups = 946 millilitre (ml)

1 gallon (US) = 768 teaspoons (tsp) = 256 tablespoons (tbsp) = 128 fluid ounces = 8 cups = 3.78 litre

1 gallon (Imperial) = 1.2 Gallon (US) = 4.54 litre

WEIGHT

In the US cooking weights are measured using pounds and ounces. This is the Avoirdupois weight and should not be confused with Troy weight or fluid ounces - which are different.

1 ounce = 28 grams

16 ounces = 1 pound = 454 grams

2.2 pounds = 1 kilogram

TEMPERATURE

In a US kitchen Fahrenheit is all that is required but in Canada both Fahrenheit and Celsius are in use even though Canada officially uses the metric system. Gas Mark is only used in the UK.

250°F = 120°C = Gas Mark ½

275°F = 135°C = Gas Mark 1

300°F = 149°C = Gas Mark 2

325°F = 162°C = Gas Mark 3

350°F = 176°C = Gas Mark 4

375°F = 190°C = Gas Mark 5

400°F = 204°C = Gas Mark 6

425°F = 218°C = Gas Mark 7

450°F = 232°C = Gas Mark 8

475°F = 246°C = Gas Mark 9

500°F = 260°C = Gas Mark 10

A GLOSSARY OF COMMON COOKING TERMS

This glossary explains some of the common cooking terms used in this book and additional terms that you may encounter in other cookbooks.

AL DENTE
An Italian term usually used to describe pasta that has been cooked so that it is still firm but not hard. It can also be used to refer to vegetables that have been cooked but still remain firm to the bite.

AU GRATIN
A dish usually prepared in a shallow casserole dish and topped with breadcrumbs, grated cheese, eggs and/or butter. It is then baked to form a browned crust on top.

BAKE
Usually means to cook in an oven using dry heat. It frequently refers to the heating (baking) of such things as bread, cakes, cookies, etc.

BARBECUE
Generally refers to grilling done outdoors or over an open charcoal or wood fire. May also refer to slow cooking with direct heat while basting with a sauce.

BASTE
Refers to keeping foods moist while cooking by coating the food (usually meat) with its own juices or with a basting sauce.

BATTER
A semi-liquid mixture, usually comprised of flour and liquid (milk, water, eggs, etc) ranging anywhere from very thin to very thick.

BEAT

Rapidly mixing, using a spoon, fork, whisk or electric mixer. This method is used to create a smooth mixture and to incorporate air into the mixture as well.

BLANCH

Immersing a fruit or vegetable into boiling water for a short time and then rapid cooling (usually in ice water) to stop the cooking process.

BLEND

Mixing two or more ingredients together until they are well combined.

BOIL

Heating a liquid until bubbles continually break the surface.

BROIL

Cooking on a grill, or under the broiler in an oven, using high, direct heat.

CARAMELIZE

Heating sugar to give it brown color and a slightly nutty flavor.

CHOP

Cutting solid ingredients, such as vegetables, into pieces using a sharp knife, cleaver or other chopping instrument.

CLARIFY

A process normally used to clarify butter. The butter is heated until the milk solids separate from the butter fat. The milk solid sink to the bottom and the clear (clarified) butter fat is poured off the top.

CREAM

To soften a fat, especially butter, by beating it at room temperature. Butter and sugar are often creamed together, making a smooth, soft paste.

DEGLAZE

Removing and dissolving food residue from the bottom of a cooking pan which was used to fry, sauté or roast some food (usually meat). To deglaze a pan, pour off any excess fat, then add some liquid. Stir the liquid, scrapping the bits from the bottom of the pan, over high heat. This is often used as the base of a gravy or sauce.

DEGREASE

Removing fat from the surface of stews, soups, or stock. The easiest way to achieve this is to cool the stew, etc. in the refrigerator and then remove the hardened fat from the surface.

DICE

Cutting food, usually vegetables, into small, uniform cubes.

DISSOLVE

Adding a dry ingredient into a liquid ingredient and mixing it so that it becomes a solution.

DREDGE

Coating moist foods with a dry ingredient prior to cooking. This is achieved by pulling or rolling moistened food through the dry coating material.

DRIZZLE

Pouring slowly and casually over the surface of a food. This direction is often used for oil, such as drizzling olive oil over a salad before tossing. Also, another example is to drizzle melted chocolate over a dessert.

DRY RUB

A dry rub is generally a mixture of salt, pepper, herbs or spices that is rubbed into meat, poultry or seafood prior to cooking.

DUST

Sprinkling food a dry ingredient such as powdered sugar.

FILLET (SOMETIMES SPELLED FILET)

When used a verb, it means to remove the bones from meat or fish. When used as a noun it refers to the piece of meat or fish that has already been boned.

FOLD

Gently incorporating a delicate ingredient into a another ingredient. This is done by hand with a large spoon or spatula by gently lifting the ingredients up from the bottom and "folding" it over the ingredient to be mixed in. Rotating the bowl while folding in the delicate ingredient helps to ensure a good mix.

Fry

Frying refers to cooking in hot fat. The amount of fat will vary depending on whether you wish to pan-fry, deep-fry or sauté. See explanations for each of those terms in this glossary.

Garnish

Garnish is used to enhance both the appearance and flavor of a dish. Garnishes include such items as vegetables, herbs, fruit, whipped cream and more.

Glaze

Glazing is to coat an ingredient with a thin sugar syrup. It also refers to a thin, pourable icing/frosting.

Grate

Using a grater to shred food into bits or shreds. Most graters have a selection of grating surfaces that will give you different sizes of bits or shreds.

Grill

Cooking on an outdoor grill, on under the broiler in the oven, using high heat. May also refer to pan grilling, such as when you make a "grilled" cheese sandwich.

Grind

Processing solids by hand or by machine to obtain tiny particles. For example, you can grind spices and coffee beans.

Julienne

Cutting vegetables, fruits, or cheeses into thin strips.

Knead

Kneading is working bread or pasta dough with the palms of your hand, or with a bread machine, to develop the gluten to achieve the proper texture.

Lukewarm

A lukewarm temperature is neither cool nor warm. Body temperature is a good rule of thumb for lukewarm.

Marinate

Soaking foods in a seasoned, frequently acidic liquid, for a period of time before cooking. This process imparts flavor and often tenderness to the food being marinated.

Mince

Chopping food into very small pieces, such as mincing garlic.

Mix

Combining ingredients by stirring.

Pan-Broil

Cooking in a hot, uncovered skillet and pouring off any fat as it develops in the pan .

Pan-Fry

Cooking in a hot, uncovered skillet in a small amount of fat.

Parboil

See "Blanch" in this glossary.

Pare

Removing the outermost skin of a fruit or vegetable.

Peel

Removing the peels from vegetables or fruits.

Pinch

A small measurement for dry ingredients such as salt. Approximately 1/16 teaspoon.

Pit

Removing the pits from fruits.

Planked

Cooking on a thick hardwood plank. Cedar planks are the most common.

Plump

Soaking dried fruits in a liquid until they are rehydrated.

Poach

Gently cooking in hot liquid that is kept just below boiling.

Proof

With today's yeast it's often not necessary to proof the yeast first. However, if you are concerned that the yeast may be old, here's how to test it:

Combine a teaspoon of sugar with about 1/2 cup of warm water (hot tap water works well, just make sure it's not too hot or that will kill the yeast).

Sprinkle the yeast on top and let it sit for about 10 minutes. If the yeast has created a bubbly foam on top of the water, then it is good.

Note: be sure to subtract the amount of water and sugar you used to proof the yeast from the amount called for in the recipe.

Punch Down

After bread dough has risen for the first time, it needs to be punched down. This is pretty much what it sounds like. You want to make sure you've removed most of the air bubbles created by the rising process. Then you can knead and shape the loaves as required and allow them to rise again.

Purée

Mashing foods until very smooth. This can be achieve by hand, using a sieve or food mill or by using a blender or food processor.

Reduce

Boiling down a liquid to reduce the volume.

Roast

Cooking in an oven using dry heat.

Sauté

Cooking food in a small amount of fat, in a shallow pan, over relatively high heat.

Scald

Bringing a liquid almost to the boiling point. The most common liquid that is scalded is milk.

Scallop

Baking a food, in a sauce or other liquid, in a casserole dish. An example is scalloped potatoes.

Score

Cutting shallow grooves in the outer surface of a food.

Sear

Browning quickly over high heat. Searing a roast before cooking it can help to keep the juices in during the roasting process.

Shred

Cutting or tearing a food, such as lettuce or cabbage, into long, narrow pieces.

Sift

Putting dry ingredients, usually flour, through a sieve or sifter. Note: with today's flours it is rarely necessary to sift.

Simmer

A simmering liquid is usually around 180° F. The surface should be fairly still, broken occasionally by a few bubbles.

Skim

Removing fat or scum from the surface of a liquid while cooking.

Steam

Cooking food about boiling water not in it, so it is the steam that cooks the food. You can use a steamer that fits in a pot or an electric steamer. Note: always be sure to check the amount of water during the steaming process to be sure it doesn't boil dry.

Steep

Extracting color and/or flavor by immersing the ingredient in almost-boiling water. An example, of course, is making tea.

Stew

Slowly simmering ingredients in a small amount of liquid for an extended period of time.

Stir

Mixing in a circular motion until the ingredients are well blended.

Toss

Combining ingredients with a lifting/dropping motion.

Whip

Beating rapidly to incorporate air into the ingredients. You can use a hand whisk or an electric mixer to whip such things as heavy cream and egg whites.

#

NEVER PAY FOR ONE OF OUR eBOOKS AGAIN

If you register your purchase of this book at

http://ebooks.geezerguides.com/

our publisher will let you know each time they have a free promotion for a new release.

The hope is that you will leave an honest review on the website where you downloaded the book. eBook sales are driven by reviews so the more favorable reviews there are from early readers the more sales we ultimately get.

It's a win win situation. New books get lots of reviews and you get to read them first and for free.

ABOUT THE AUTHORS

Geoff and Vicky Wells split their time between Ontario, Canada and the island of Eleuthera in the Bahamas. They maintain several websites including GeezerGuides.com which was originally set up for Baby Boomers but has now morphed into the publisher of an eclectic collection of these little booklets.

More information than you could possibly want to know about them is available on their blog http://www.geoffandvickywells.com

For more books in this series visit

http://ebooks.geezerguides.com/

65648712R00078

Made in the USA
San Bernardino, CA
05 January 2018